D0190920

THE GOSPEL'S TRIUMPH OVER COMMUNISM

THE GOSPEL'S TRIUMPH OVER COMMUNISM

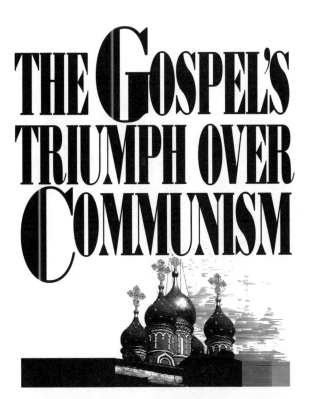

MICHAEL BOURDEAUX

BETHANY HOUSE PUBLISHERS
Minneapolis, Minnesota 55438

Published by Bethany House Publishers
A Ministry of Bethany Fellowship, Inc.
6820 Auto Club Road, Minneapolis, Minnesota 55438

Printed in the United States of America

Library of Congress Cataloging-in-Publication Data

Bourdeaux, Michael
    [Gorbachev, glasnost & the Gospel]
    The Gospel's triumph over communism / Michael Bourdeaux.

    Reprint. Originally published: London : Hodder and Stoughton, 1990.
    Includes bibliographical references and index.

    1. Persecution—Soviet Union—History. 2. Soviet Union—Church history—1917–   3. Communism and Christianity—Soviet Union—History. 4. Church and state—Soviet Union—History. 5. Freedom of religion—Soviet Union—History. I. Title.
BR1608.S65B684   1991
274.7'0828—dc20   91-18301
ISBN 1-55661-228-1   CIP

To Lara Clare

Acknowledgments

It has been a great privilege to write the substance of this book back in Oxford after thirty years away, so my first thanks go to the Leverhulme Trust, whose financial assistance made this possible. My old college, St Edmund Hall, welcomed me graciously as a Visiting Fellow and St Antony's College elected me as a Senior Associate Member, enabling me to benefit from the stimulus of their lecture programme.

The Trust provided me also with a research assistant, Suzanne Oliver, without whose tireless work I would not have finished in double the time. She has been my mind-reader and critic, but has provided considerable original material of her own, particularly for Chapter 5. The amount of information was overwhelming: perhaps enough is left over for a book to follow up each chapter. The staff at Keston College in Kent have gathered this material day by day and it reposes there in the archive.

The idea for the book came from Juliet Newport, whose encouragement and insight at Hodder and Stoughton saw the book through from first to last.

I am grateful to several people for helpful suggestions, particulary Professor Sir Dimitri Obolensky and Professor Archie Brown of Oxford University, and Michael Rowe, Jane Ellis, John Anderson and others at Keston College.

Professor and Mrs John Fennell and Lady Joya Roberts provided havens of peace in Oxford and generous refreshment along the way.

Most of all I once again pay tribute to the inspiration of those Christians in the Soviet Union, contact with whom over the years has never failed to inspire and enrich.

Michael Bourdeaux   March 1990
Iffley, Oxford

Contents

Photographs

Fr Alexander Men (*Keston College*)
Fr Tavrion (*Keston College*)
Boris Talantov (*Aid to Russian Christians*)
The laying of a foundation stone (*Jim Forest*)
Millennium press conference (*NCCC-USA*)
The Danilov Monastery (*NCCC-USA*)
Archbishop Kirill of Smolensk (*Jim Forest*)
Archbishop Chrysostom of Irkutsk (*Jim Forest*)
Alexander Ogorodnikov (*Cahiers du Samizdat*)
Metropolitan Filaret of Kiev (*Jim Forest*)
Viktor Popkov (*James Stark*)
Fr Gleb Yakunin (*Keston College*)
Deacon Vladimir Rusak (*Aid to Russian Christians*)
Church Council (*Jim Forest*)
The unofficial exhibitions of photographs (*Keston College*)
Fifty Christian volunteer workers (*Aid to Russian Christians*)
Baptism in River Dnieper, Kiev (*Aid to the Persecuted*)
Alexander Semchenko (*Keston College*)
Ivan Fedotov (*Keston College*)
Celebrations of Odessa unregistered Baptist church (*Aid to Russian Christians*)
Valeri Barinov (*Keston College*)
Nijole Sadunaite (*Keston College*)
Bishop Julijonas Steponavicius (*Keston College*)
Bishop Pavlo Vasylyk (*Ukrainian Catholic Church*)
Ivan Hel (*John Hands*)
Procession of bishops at Lviv demonstration (*Keston College*)
Iosyp Terelya (*Ukrainian Catholic Church*)
Wife and grand-daughter of Ivan Hel (*Bill Hampson/Jubilee Campaign*)
Young Baptist volunteer (*Keston College*)

Introduction

When I was doing the research for this book in 1989, Mikhail Sergeyevich Gorbachev was soaring on eagle's wings above the political lowlands of the world. The acme of his flight should have been the Nobel Peace Prize awarded him in December 1990, yet by that time not only had his stock fallen low enough to occasion considerable international criticism of his leadership, but domestically he was under such pressure that he announced his unwillingness to go to Norway for the event.

The period of almost five years since his accession to office had been punctuated by a series of triumphant foreign visits, during which he had received increasing acclaim as the man who had changed the course of late twentieth-century history. The Oslo event, one expected, would have provided him with the most glittering accolade and placed him in the most universal forum of any of them. Yet, disappointing thousands of foreign guests, he punctured the event by hiding out in Moscow, sending a deputy to undertake the task of replacing the irreplaceable.

What had gone wrong? The citation for the Peace Prize drew attention to the new order in East-West relations which Gorbachev had inaugurated, a new security in Europe, indeed the liberation of over a hundred million people in Eastern and Central Europe from the 'yoke of communism.' The citation did not quite use this inflammatory terminology, and certainly conservative elements in the Soviet Union, beginning with the KGB, would have been even more infuriated if it had. But infuriated they certainly were: not so much at the Nobel Prize itself but at the whole process of disintegration of empire which by the middle of 1990 was clearly irreversible.

Even reforming Soviet opinion, of which Mr Gorbachev had been the unchallenged front runner up to 1988, had begun to desert him. He had promised so much, but his citizens faced only empty shelves and increasing crime in the heartland of the Soviet cities. Immediately on publication of the original edition of this book in Britain (September 1990), I went to a conference in Leningrad on human rights, taking copies with me. The British edition had a bright red cover framing a striking picture of Gorbachev himself. The people I met were all sympathetic to the subject of religious liberty itself; they acknowledged that Gorbachev had brought a freedom to their lives they at one time could never even have dreamed of, yet revulsion at the colour of communism and at the smiling face was the emotion every single person expressed.

Outside the Soviet Union, the pendulum of world public opinion was now beginning to swing away from Mr Gorbachev, as his *perestroika* programme was manifestly foundering and the country was beginning to slide inexorably into economic chaos compounded by ceaseless ethnic conflicts. The Soviet republics, with the Baltic States commanding a great deal of international sympathy, were clearly not going to be permitted any political freedoms comparable to those now enjoyed by Poland, East Germany, Czechoslovakia and Hungary. It was reappraisal time. Had Mr Gorbachev really intended to be the architect of a new world order? Perhaps, having seen that the empire was no longer sustainable, he introduced tactics which constituted a series of desperate moves to save the heartland of communism, making his oft-proclaimed ideal of 'democratisation' a highly dubious one. Or had he genuinely flown high on the wings of reform, only to have them clipped by the old guard, an alliance of the KGB and the army, when he returned to their company?

The episode of the resignation of Eduard Shevardnadze, the highly regarded foreign minister, was ominous. Less than two weeks after Mr Gorbachev should have gone to Oslo, Shevardnadze's unheralded announcement to the Soviet parliament stunned the world. The terms of his speech, in which he claimed that the Soviet Union was sliding into dictatorship, were provocative enough. Later it emerged that this was no mere protest on principle. The ancient powers had summoned him and threatened him in something like these terms: You pulled us out of the war in Afghanistan, where we were taking a principled stand in the communist cause; you prevented us from making a pre-emptive strike against the so-called democratic insurgents in East Germany, Czechoslovakia and elsewhere, so the communist cause of decades has been undone in a few weeks; now you have forced us to betray our old allies, the Iraqis, and you are pulling us into the Gulf conflict on the wrong side. You had better reverse your policies or else. . . .

Following this, the sequence of events was even more ominous. Under cover of the diversion of the world's attention to the Middle East, those same forces of darkness moved into the Baltic States and murdered defenders of freedom in Lithuania and Latvia. A month after the ceremony, the winner of the Nobel Peace Prize had blood on his hands. Or perhaps, as he claimed, he was not responsible? No matter. If these had been acts of insubordination by the armed forces, court martial of the culprits should inevitably have followed, as they unquestionably would if, for example, defenceless people had been mown down in Northern Ireland. The guilt, ultimately, is Gorbachev's.

We now come to the key question which arises on the occasion of the American publication of this book, almost a year after its original appearance in the UK. How appropriate is it to publish a work, in virtually its original form, in which many pages celebrate a hero whose image has subsequently become tarnished?

The answer is relatively simple. We are not writing hagiography to venerate a saint. We are recording chapters in the Christian history of the late Twentieth Century. Even if this very day the Soviet Union should collapse in chaos and bloodshed, the liberation of Christianity, of religion in general, after seventy years of systematic persecution under the law will continue to deserve the attention of future historians and the praise of new generations of the faithful. It is not so much the opening of the prison doors which we note, though this was dramatic enough, but rather the spontaneous rejection by millions (in Eastern and Central Europe, as well as in the Soviet Union) of a uniform communist materialism in favour of the spiritual dimension in any of its multiplicity of forms.

Unquestionably, this was a turning point in Christian history though it is as yet far too early to see it in perspective. The process of rejection was well underway long before the advent of Mr Gorbachev. There is no justification whatsoever for giving him credit, as some commentators have done, for the religious revival itself. Previous books of mine trace the origins of this back at least to the 1960s, possibly earlier.

Nevertheless, Mr Gorbachev was an enabler, even one in his early days in power of spirit, courage and vision. Had I been consulted about his Nobel Prize – say, in October 1990 – I would have said yes – but with a citation making reference to his reversal of old Soviet repressive policies towards democratic and dissident movements and especially the fulfillment of his 1988 promise of a new law on religion.

This book, therefore, is not only a record of a significant moment in Christian history: more importantly, it proves decisively that even in our secular age the ways of God are more powerful than the most systematic machinations of the mind of man.

April 1991

1 The Crisis of History

For the first time in history, a state attempted, for seventy years, to eradicate all concept of God from society. Regimes in the past have misused religion in every conceivable way, enforcing the worship of idols, relentlessly persecuting those who raised altars to other deities and marching off to war against the infidel under the flag of their own god. Never before, however, had men stood up and said, 'There are no gods in our state; mankind has all the potential within himself; science, equality and economic progress hold the key to the future.'

In 1988, Soviet leaders not only realised they had failed, but they put the process into reverse. This book recounts how it happened and what the consequences have been.

The reinstatement of God in the Kremlin – at one point literally, when the Patriarch celebrated the liturgy in the Cathedral of the Dormition – preceded the collapse of communism in Central and Eastern Europe in a way that is slightly more than symbolic. Christianity, in a different way in every one of those countries, is now a force in the affairs of the nation and therefore of the world.

The inability to comprehend this aspect of culture under communism – the enforcement of atheist dogma – inhibits the West from fully understanding the processes which are now occurring. Western church leaders, commentating on the Soviet Union throughout the seventy years of its history, more often than not lacked the insight to interpret events with a prophetic word. One prominent Western theologian, confronted with one of the first lists of Baptist prisoners in the Soviet Union in the early 1960s, held it up before a meeting of the Central Committee of the World Council of Churches and asked, 'What are 200 prisoners in a country of 200 million people?' By this he intended to say that there was freedom enough for believers in Russia. There was no need to break the law and those who did so were troublemakers. He had missed the prophetic element in the conduct of those men and women. He had assumed that the Christian norm should be a general acceptance of the society around them.

Such attitudes to some extent permeated Western thinking. Some new social experiment was taking place in the East. There were a thousand obstacles on the road and individual non-conformists were still being sacrificed to the Gulag, but overall there was progress and a general acceptance that, in the words of George Bernard Shaw on his return from the Soviet Union, 'I have seen the future, I have been there.' Despite some excellent reporting by journalists from Moscow over many years and the abundance of publications on such topics as the abuse of psychiatry for political ends and the prevalence of religious persecution, there was little real understanding of the indignity visited on human beings by the communist system, leading eventually to their rejection of it.

The old way of looking at the world as a confrontation between two massive power blocs, with the third world suffering as a result, has disappeared. There are few human beings on earth whose lives are not potentially affected in one way or the other – especially those who continue to live under other oppressive regimes. The perspective for religion in the new era is transformed. Early in 1990 a sage of our generation, Lord Jakobovits, reflected on these events thus:

> What is taking place is of seismic dimensions and there is more to it than just liberalizing. The collapse of communism itself will be a major factor in bringing back the religious influence in world affairs. It means the collapse of the view that the essential features of human progress were of a materialistic nature. It provides the present religious leadership with a more exciting contemporary challenge than they have had in the past.[1]

Another consequence of our misunderstanding of communist society is that only those in the West bold enough to face the accusation of being cold war warriors dared expose the true nature of communism – and for a Christian this led to exclusion from the mainstream of acceptance, at least in some church circles. It is still somehow an unpopular view to rate Stalin as a worse tyrant than Hitler. Zbigniew Brzezinski, formerly President Carter's National Security Adviser, reckons that communism in one form or another cost the lives of fifty million people, counting those whose deaths were consequent upon mistaken political or economic decisions, as well as the victims of direct persecution. Stalin therefore has no rival as the greatest tyrant in human history. In his book, *The Grand Failure*, written in 1988 and published in the USA early in 1989, well before the cracks in the Berlin Wall opened into the fissures which destroyed the system, Brzezinski spectacularly predicted the imminent fall of communism. In 1988 he delivered a précis of his views at the Hugh Seton Watson Memorial Lecture in London before an astonished and partly sceptical audience.

Too many people in the West, and perhaps especially Christians, who should have known better, simply failed to appreciate the totality with which communism in practice rejected every proven human and religious value, stripping men and women of trust in each other, excising any sense of individual responsibility for the destiny of society, robbing people of their future, just as the rewriting of history had robbed them of their past. It is impossible for anyone who does not know the Soviet system well to appreciate the extent of the deprivation which believers have experienced. Therefore it is difficult, without a great effort of the imagination, to start on the right wavelength to enable one to appreciate the scale of the changes which Mr Gorbachev's policies have brought into religious life.

Churches – Open and Closed

Even in these days of *glasnost*, it is impossible to assess the full extent of Stalin's persecution of religious believers, their persons, their beliefs, their institutions. So many died in the general purges and famines that no figures can be extracted to indicate those who were victims primarily because of their faith. In Stalin's Russia simply to be a priest warranted a prison sentence which, in its turn, was often the equivalent of a death sentence.

Even in the midst of such horror, there was an act of violence against property which Soviet believers would never forgive: the systematic closure and destruction of the churches. Often they were the only stone construction in a locality where dwellings were wooden, so the ready-made policy was to commandeer them as agricultural stores or use them to house the village club or cinema, after removing all the crosses and any other visible symbols of the faith. But it is not so easy to make a church look like a barn, especially a Russian one, with its onion domes and elevated walls. As Solzhenitsyn so vividly put it:

> When you travel the by-roads of Central Russia you begin to understand the secret of the pacifying Russian countryside. It is in the churches. They trip up the slopes, ascend the high hills, come down to the broad rivers, like princesses in white and red, they lift their bell-towers – graceful, shapely, variegated – high over mundane timber and thatch, they nod to each other from afar, from villages that are cut off and invisible to

each other they soar to the same heaven. And wherever you wander in the fields or meadows, however far from habitation, you are never alone: from over the hayricks, the wall of trees, and even the curve of the earth's surface, the head of some bell-tower will beckon you from Borki Lovetskiye, Lyubichi or Gavrilovskoye.

But when you reach the village you find that not the living, but the dead greeted you from afar. The crosses were knocked off the roof or twisted out of place long ago. The dome has been stripped and there are gaping holes between its rusty ribs. Weeds grow on the roofs and in the cracks in the walls. Usually the graveyard has been neglected, its crosses flattened and the graves churned up. Over the years rain has penetrated to the murals over the altar and obscene inscriptions are scrawled over them.

In the porch there are barrels of lubricating oil and a tractor is turning in towards them, or a lorry has backed into the church doorway to pick up some sacks. One church reverberates to the shudder of lathes, another is locked and silent. In others various groups and clubs are meeting: 'Aim at high milk yields!' 'A poem on peace.' 'A heroic deed.'

People were always selfish and often unkind, but the evening chimes would ring out, floating over villages, fields and woods, reminding people to abandon the trivial concerns of this world and give time and thought to eternity . . . our forefathers put all that was finest in themselves, all their understanding of life into these stones, into these bell-towers.

Ram it in, Vitka, give it a bash, don't be afraid! Film show at six, dancing at eight![2]

Solzhenitsyn had not openly declared himself as a Christian at the time when he wrote these words (about 1961), but the outrage which he felt at this desecration of Russia's heritage was shared by the two generations since Lenin. By the time he wrote, Khrushchev's policies were again further devastating churches in the countryside. These buildings made a statement about Russia's past and were a symbol of hope for the future – hardly surprising, then, that the local authorities wished to eradicate them. For ordinary believers the struggle for freedom of religion has usually focused on the longing to win back their place of worship. They were not impressed by the handful of churches converted into museums and shown off with pride to demonstrate the glory of old Russian architecture.

By the outbreak of the Second World War only a few hundred churches throughout the Soviet Union were open for worship. However, so desperate was Stalin for support in the war effort that he encouraged the Russian Orthodox Church to collaborate with him and rewarded it for doing so. This led to the return of several thousand churches in the 1940s which were lovingly and carefully restored by believers, a process which took many years because of the universal shortage of building materials. To these were added many more in the lands conquered by the Red Army as the Nazis retreated; they had not formerly been on Soviet soil and had therefore not undergone persecution.

By 1959 the church had returned to some kind of regular life, at least by Soviet standards, and the public face of Christianity was more normal than it had been at any time since the Revolution. This, then, made Khrushchev's renewed campaign all the more devastating. It coincided with my arrival in Moscow as a member of the first-ever British Council exchange in a country where no students from Western countries had ever spent a length of time.

I was able, therefore, gradually to gauge the atmosphere among believers. This took time, because there were no believers at all, at least overt ones, in the university where I was studying. However, by then even the newspapers were beginning to announce that churches were closing again and trials of believers as enemies of the state were reported with attendant accusations of drunkenness, homosexuality, robbery and embezzlement. Monasticism almost ceased to exist and the Soviet Union's theological seminaries were reduced from eight in number to three.

Khrushchev's persecution of religion stood out more sharply, because in other ways society was moving in a more liberal direction, following the denunciation of Stalin at the Twentieth Party Congress in 1956. There has never been an explanation of why believers were singled out and treated with a savagery which would have undermined Mr Khrushchev's benign image round the world, had this policy become better known. Most likely the ideologues in the Kremlin were dismayed at what Khrushchev had done and put him under severe pressure. To justify himself as a true communist, he attacked the enemy in the midst – and a defenceless one at that – claiming that the Soviet Union was well on the way to attaining communism and there would be no place for religion in the ideal state of the future.

No one in these early days of Khrushchev had ever heard of Solzhenitsyn and it seemed at first that no voice could be heard expressing the outrage that millions felt at this assault. A phrase often used at the time was 'the church of silence', but the improvement in the life of the ordinary believer in the post-war years, followed by the death of Stalin in 1953, gradually gave people the courage to overcome the fear born of the new terror. The church did not suffer the renewed persecution in silence. At first the voices were isolated, apparently crying in the wilderness. It was my privilege to be the person *in situ*, but with the outside contacts, to pick up their distant signals and eventually, as the work of Keston College developed, to transmit them to the world. The task was always to focus the antennae in the right direction and to pick out the true voice from the torrent of propaganda which official church representatives presented after 1961 in such forums as the World Council of Churches and the Prague Christian Peace Conference.

While no one would assert that Christian protest was the sole motivator of an emergent human rights movement, it unquestionably played a role which academic research, even to this day, has never fully acknowledged. Soon the intelligentsia would protest over the trial of the authors Andrei Sinyavsky and Yuli Daniel, who had evaded the literary straitjacket by sending their satirical works abroad for publication under a pseudonym. Even Jewish protest, which for many people came to symbolise the human rights movement in the Soviet Union, did not emerge until almost a decade after isolated Christians had first begun to call for justice.

The Russian and Ukrainian Baptists, about whom we shall say more in Chapter 6, were the very first to co-ordinate their protests and by April 1965 Gennadi Kryuchkov and Georgi Vins had made the first detailed analysis of the injustices of Soviet legislation.[3] The drive and co-ordination of this movement, which rapidly broke away from the Moscow-dominated and officially registered structure when its demands received a blank rebuttal, remains unique even today in the clarity of its legal formulations in campaigning for justice. The scrutiny to which they subjected the existing processes for the regulation of church–state relations was a model for any human rights movement, though its influence remained relatively limited, because the Baptists did not have many connections with mainstream activism. However, there was one group right outside their normal range of contacts with which the Baptists did establish useful relations, the circle around Gleb Yakunin, which later became the Christian Committee for the Defence of Believers' Rights.

If any one man or woman in the Soviet Union embodies the Christian's cry for a new deal, the ability to organise other people to achieve it and the readiness of that individual to suffer in the process, it is Fr Gleb. He comes from a religious family, but lost his faith after the war, at the age of fifteen, under the influence of communist propaganda. His yearning for an open air life led him to become a student of forestry at Irkutsk, Siberia, where he came under the influence of one of Russia's great Orthodox evangelists, Fr Alexander Men. In the age of *perestroika* Fr Alexander frequently addressed a whole roomful of atheists and 'seekers', holding them spellbound for up to three hours (a videotape is available, showing him doing this). Back in the days of Stalin or Khrushchev, it was infinitely more dangerous to wean a young man away from some technical institute and into the ordained ministry, but this is what happened with Fr Gleb, showing that the religious revival, at least in a modest form, goes back to the immediate post-war years.

Fr Gleb's temporary break with the church ensured that he returned to it with renewed zeal. He came to Moscow determined to seek ordination. His mother told him to finish his forestry studies first, which he did, by which time he had married Iraida, who was to prove his faithful consort during a life of great testing. Only with great difficulty did he manage to pursue his theological studies, because he was exactly the sort of young man that the state was concerned to keep out of the seminary, but even in those days there were some brave bishops who were set on helping those who had a true vocation. Fr Gleb's mentor was Archbishop Leonid of Mozhaisk, later Metropolitan of Riga.

Ordination followed in 1962, but his work as a dedicated parish priest in Moscow lasted only for a brief spell, for this was now the heyday of the Khrushchev persecution. Knowing both the provinces and the capital city as he did, and rapidly acquiring a reputation as a fearless preacher at a time when most proclamation of the Gospel stopped well short of any practical application to an atheist society, Fr Gleb found that people visiting Moscow from distant corners of the Soviet Union sometimes made their way to his church. The tales they brought with them were horrifying: closure of churches by the local authorities in disregard of all the legal norms, brutal treatment of those who tried to resist, frequent imprisonment of believers after rigged trials.

Fr Gleb began to collect such information systematically and the word soon spread that he was the person to contact. Before long he and a fellow-priest, Fr Nikolai Eshliman, had compiled a considerable dossier. He quietly sounded out one or two older priests, asking the question why no one was willing to take an open stand against this new policy of the state. Eleven or so people said they were prepared to do something, but the promised solidarity failed to materialise, as a result of pressure from the KGB. Just one bishop made his own representations. From others there was always the same answer: 'It's wiser to keep quiet. The storm will pass. Speaking out will only make things worse.'

However, Fr Gleb's temperament would not allow him to watch others suffer in silence, particularly when people were approaching him for help. The initiative he and Fr Nikolai took was bold and unprecedented. In November and December 1965 they wrote two lengthy and detailed letters summarising the facts they had collected, setting them in a legal framework reminiscent of the Baptists' initiative of earlier in the year. They addressed one to the Soviet Government requesting justice and the other to the Patriarch begging him to speak out in defence of the persecuted church.

A quarter of a century later it is almost impossible to indicate just how brave this unprecedented action was. Except for the Baptists, no one in any field had ever defied the Soviet Government in such an open or organised way. Instead of bringing them to trial and imprisoning them alongside those they were trying to defend, the authorities leaned upon the Patriarch to act in their stead. The two priests were suspended from their parishes and subjected to an injunction of silence. Yet this in no way dimmed the impact of what they had done. Their words looked at again in the Gorbachev era read like a blueprint for church *perestroika*:

> No less than ten thousand churches and dozens of monasteries have been closed [during the Khrushchev campaign], among which we should specially mention the Monastery of the Caves at Kiev, the most ancient sacred place of our Orthodox people . . . Moreover, we consider it our right as citizens to call your attention to the undeniable fact that the mass closure of churches, a campaign instigated from above, has created an atmosphere of anti-religious fanaticism which has led to the barbaric destruction of a large number of superb and unique works of art.[4]

During his ten years of silence, a self-effacing act of ecclesiastical obedience, Fr Gleb watched the Brezhnev era become established. Whatever modest hopes accompanied its early years soon evaporated. Its economic policies moved nowhere and Mr Gorbachev later called the resulting mess the period of 'stagnation' (*zastoi*). In the field of human rights and culture, the writers' trials set the tone. Although it may have seemed, from the outside at least, that vigorous persecution of the church had subsided, persecution on the 'administrative' level became the main tool employed by the state in restricting church activity during this time. Churches found it difficult to register their communities, buildings were closed on the slightest pretext and there were petty restrictions at all levels – for example the refusal to provide electricity supplies to church buildings. Close monitoring of church activity was maintained at all levels. Active Christians continued to face difficulties in embarking upon or completing higher education or finding jobs in their chosen field. All of these factors combined showed how believers would continue to be treated as second class citizens: where there was not outright persecution, believers faced universal discrimination.

This era did, however, see increased 'dissident' and human rights activity, no doubt spurred on by the Helsinki agreements of 1975 as such issues began to feature more prominently on the international agenda. There was a crack-down in the republics against nationalism and in prison nationalists found themselves alongside Baptist activists, writers and Jews, as well as an assortment of political prisoners who refused to keep silent. In 1979 and 1980 the arrest and trial took place of religious activists such as Alexander Ogorodnikov, with others who had become involved in his unofficial Christian discussion group, the 'Christian Seminar'.

Among them were Christian activists from all the main denominations. Fr Gleb Yakunin had become their champion, acting with his supporters old and new to establish in 1976 the Christian Committee for Believers' Rights. This time the emphasis was more on ecumenical action. The documents he collected came from various denominations, again representing the most remote geographical areas of the Soviet Union. He did this after he had written an open letter to the Fifth General Assembly of the World Council of Churches in Nairobi begging for help for the persecuted church from the whole international Christian community. The debate which his letter provoked led him to believe – wrongly, as it turned out – that the WCC was behind him. His energy was prodigious. He collected no fewer than 423 documents, totalling nearly 3,000 pages, most of which he managed to send abroad, a record of contemporary church history in the USSR and of state persecution which could never be rivalled. He added to his growing world reputation by including Jews in his defence of religious rights.

By 1979 the lack of support from his own hierarchy and the unyielding attitude of the state led Fr Gleb to throw out a challenge which seemed to many at the time to be preposterous, but which now appears to have been totally justified: believers who wished to evade the straitjacket of state control should deliberately create unregistered – and therefore illegal – parishes and there should be secret ordination of clergy to set up a church structure parallel to the Moscow Patriarchate, but free of its domination.

The authorities could no longer tolerate such a firebrand and they came for him on 1 November 1979. Ten months later they sentenced him to ten years, five in labour camp, five in exile. His trial even more clearly indicated that Brezhnev had started a pointed drive against all democratic activity and many other human rights activists were soon to follow him to gaol.

Fr Gleb Yakunin served over eight years of his sentence before being released a little early in 1987 as a result of the new *perestroika*. During those years of silence, punctuated only by one or two letters smuggled out of the camps, including one begging me to intercede with the Soviet Government and with world opinion to allow him to have a Bible, he did not lose his symbolic status. He and a few others like him had done much to restore the moral authority of Russian Orthodoxy for those of the younger generation seeking a guiding principle in life. Without the likes of Fr Gleb the ground would not have been prepared for the period of church *perestroika* which followed his release.

Incredible as it may seem, there were three times as many churches open on the day Stalin died as when Gorbachev came to power in 1985. This is due solely to Khrushchev's destruction of the churches, not to the mass abandonment of the faith which propagandists claimed.

From 1987 the Soviet press began to publish articles in which believers in many different parts of the country demanded the reopening of their churches. This was still the focus of the aspirations of millions: to have an open church in which to pray and sing the liturgy celebrated clearly and reverently by their own priest. The press not only began in an unprecedented way to reflect the feelings of believers; it actually became a forum for them and unquestionably caused many who would never have dared to act in this way openly to campaign for change.

One of the most amazing examples of this was in *Moscow News*, which became a mouthpiece for *glasnost*. Alexander Nezhny, a campaigning journalist who would later identify himself as a Christian, wrote an indictment of the current policy of refusing to allow new churches to open, even where the building still existed, following its earlier confiscation. He wrote (the words are original, from the English-language version of the publication):

Before 1962, Kirov had two Russian Orthodox Church communities, two churches – St. Feodor and St. Serafim. In 1962, in line with the then official policy that we should enter communism (which was believed to be close at hand) without religious people, or at least with a minimal quantity of such, St. Feodor Church was closed and its parish disbanded. Because the city authorities had rebuilding plans for the riverside, the church on the Vyatka bank was torn down. The plans called for erecting in its place a monument celebrating the city's 600th anniversary. But the intriguing plan has so far given us only an ugly concrete slab buried under which is a capsule with a message to future generations.

An irreverent thought came to me when I faced the slab. For some unaccountable reason I thought that our wiser descendants would feel uneasy because of our desire to project a better image of ourselves than that which exists. I thought it would have been much more fair and moral to leave a two-word message buried in the high bank – 'Forgive us!' – because we have failed to preserve here, on the bank of the Vyatka, either St. Feodor Church or the striking [sic] beautiful seventeenth-century cathedral.[5]

These words, as a harbinger of church *perestroika*, would have been impressive enough in any context as early as August 1987 when they appeared. However, an additional and very special circumstance gave them an extraordinary resonance. When Fr Gleb Yakunin began his campaign in 1965 and ensured that his open letters were published in the West, one of the few people to give him open allegiance was a layman, Boris Talantov, a mathematics teacher from that very city of Kirov, formerly called Vyatka before the communists renamed it after a Party hero. In 1966 Talantov had written:

In the period 1960–63 the Kirov regional officials of the Council for Russian Orthodox Church Affairs [now called the Council for Religious Affairs] . . . arbitrarily removed 21 of the 80 priests active in 1959 and registered no-one in their place . . . At the same time the regional executive committee would pass a resolution to close the church and it would assign the building to the local *kolkhoz* or town *soviet* . . . When liquidating places of worship there would be a show of brute force. This would be carried out under the protection of the militia and auxiliary police, often at night. Believers would be forbidden to enter the church. The valuables would be removed without any inventory being made. In the Kirov region, when places of worship were liquidated, the interiors would always be barbarically destroyed, icons and holy vessels burned and all the valuables stolen . . .

Thus in the autumn of 1962 the congregation of St. Feodor's Church in Kirov was, with the agreement of the clergy, merged with St. Serafim's Church. The building itself was then destroyed and thrown into the river Vyatka. At the beginning of 1964 Bishop Ioann of Kirov shut the prayer house in the settlement of Rudnichnoye, which had been built by believers themselves in 1947. Officially this was described as merging one church with another situated forty kilometres away![6]

Six months after Boris Talantov had written his lengthy indictment, no less detailed and documented than Fr Gleb Yakunin's of two years earlier and of which we have quoted only the briefest extract, the local newspaper, *Kirovskaya pravda*, launched into a savage attack. Metropolitan Nikodim, then the chief spokesman for the Russian Orthodox Church, chimed in and claimed during a visit to London that Talantov's letter was anonymous, was therefore untrustworthy and should be disregarded. Under the immense strain of interrogations, accusations and criticism from the church leadership itself, Talantov's wife collapsed and died in September 1967. He himself was arrested two years later, though by this time a sick old man, and sentenced to two years' imprisonment under Article 190–1 (anti-Soviet slander). He did not live to regain his freedom. Betrayed by his own bishops, he died alone in a prison hospital on 4 January 1971. This did not prevent a large crowd from attending his funeral in Kirov. His death showed that nothing had changed under Brezhnev. In 1987 he and his work were reinstated in all but name in the Soviet press itself. Over the next few months there would be a spate of articles reporting demands of believers for the reopening of their churches all over the Soviet Union.

Clearly, religion never came anywhere near to dying out and Stalin was mistaken in thinking that closure of a church or imprisonment of a priest would lead to the demise of the faith in any given area. Nevertheless, systematic persecution eradicated virtually every Christian institution in the land, and the devastation will take generations to repair. Broadly speaking, religious revival can take two forms: first, the restoration of the formal life of the churches, flourishing worship, lively theological education, the publication of Christian literature – these we will discuss presently; and second, the restoration of religious values in society – a trend much harder to monitor.

Restoration of Religious Values

In a very real sense, religious values never died out, even in the years of the most brutal repression. It is hardly coincidental that Alexander Blok, poet of the Revolution, became a Christian at the end of his life. All four of his greatest successors embraced the faith in one way or another and kept it alive between the wars, even though they could not publish their works at the time. Mandelstam, Akhmatova, Tsvetaeva and Pasternak upheld values which communism could suppress, but not eradicate.

The war saw overt Christian revival, with Stalin needing the support of the churches when the Nazis were overrunning the Soviet Union.

The reopening of thousands of churches sent a signal that at some time society would again be able to acknowledge religious values.

The lifting of the terror after Khrushchev's secret speech of 1956 permitted people to begin discussing their feelings and aspirations more openly, if tentatively. Then followed the renewed persecution, the closure of churches, the response of believers, the imprisonment of those who defended the faith. In the absence of any significant official Christian publishing, the resulting circulation of manuscripts, typescripts and sometimes even beautifully home-bound books (*samizdat*) played an incalculable role in this rediscovery of belief. With a few exceptions, the new martyrs did not die for their faith, but they witnessed to it steadfastly in the prisons and camps. After their release their renewed presence revitalised their own communities and impressed literally tens of thousands of young people, who were beginning to be sickened by the inculcation of mindless atheism as a central part of their education in school.

In 1977 I visited a secret Sunday school in Kiev. The teacher had just been released from prison. Young, attractive, fearless, she risked further imprisonment by recounting her experiences to a group of fourteen- to sixteen-year-olds who hung on her every word:

> When I was in prison the language during every waking hour was foul and appalling. Sometimes we went to the punishment cells for proclaiming the Gospel to these poor lost souls, these criminals who had often fallen into sin simply because nobody had ever held the ideal of Christ before them. But we sometimes needed a rest from punishment. Then we would simply smile at their curses. When we came into a room where they were, they would know at once that we belonged to Christ because they could hear a tone of love in our voices. Children, you have to face mockery in school every day from your teachers and fellow-students. But you don't need to be punished every single day. Just show people your faith by the radiance on your faces, even when you're not saying a word.

The lesson continued for nearly an hour, unbroken by singing or by question and answer. Never before or since have I observed boys and girls of that age group so utterly absorbed in listening to a single voice. The suffering the teacher had herself so recently undergone endowed her with a moral authority which knit those young people together in a shared experience.

Gradually in recent years published literature, the cinema, and more recently the general press, have expressed an interest in religious themes, leading in the time of *glasnost* to what one can only call a rehabilitation of Christian values in the media. It is a fascinating story.

The very first example of this was as early as 1962, curiously enough at the time when the persecution under Khrushchev was at its worst. He personally sanctioned the publication of Solzhenitsyn's *One Day in the Life of Ivan Denisovich*, mainly to justify the accusations which he had made against Stalin. Here was an autobiographical account of prison-camp life which riveted just about every literate person in the Soviet Union. It did not escape this vast readership that there were two unforgettable portrayals of Christians in it: Alyosha, the Baptist, who told Ivan Denisovich the way a believer must pray; and a nameless priest who treats every meal as a sacrament, appearing as an icon of Christ as, with immense dignity, he unfolds his scrap of clean cloth on the filthy table before laying his hunk of bread on it and keeping his head upright while he takes his soup spoon to his mouth, just as every Orthodox believer does when he receives communion.

In the Brezhnev years this kind of writing could not develop, but the hiatus was gradually broken by the emergence of a group of writers who have been called the *derevenshchiki* (men of the countryside), who began to write naturalistically and with reverence about the persistence of old customs, among which, of course, religion had its place. Believers, although old, simple and often illiterate, gradually emerge as good people. There was plenty of criticism in the hard-line ideological journals of the Party, but this did not lead to suppression of these works. Gradually religion seemed to be seeping out of the confines of the scattered churches and back into the fabric of society.

Daniil Granin is a novelist who has always displayed a high moral purpose and would later, in Gorbachev's day, make an influential plea for a return to moral standards in society (see p.189). Here is a paragraph from his novel *The Picture*, describing a minor official and member of the Party (Losev) who takes his girlfriend to a town where they are not known. They visit the cathedral as tourists:

> It was the first time Losev had been inside a big, working church while a service was going on . . . The proceedings at the altar – the appearances and disappearances of the white-clad servers, the deacon swinging his censer, the procession of young priests in their brocade robes – it all seemed vaguely familiar, and he began remembering words he had never used and did not even know he knew . . . There must be something in all this, he thought: in the smoky gilded faces on the icons, in the resonance within the dome, in his own reflections about the shortness of life here on earth and about what is to follow that life.[7]

Losev is deeply impressed with the service, but is determined not to succumb to the lure of the faith. His schoolteacher girlfriend, Tanya, has less resistance and comes out of church on the brink of belief. She tells him that she has been praying, even though she did not know how to go about it. Later they talk to one of the servers from the church, who maintains that the way to faith is through doubt and recommends reading the Book of Job as a vehicle for bringing a doubter to the faith.

This is already a long step from the sentimental portrayal of believers as ageing and simple people. It is hard to believe that this novel saw the light of day in 1980, while Brezhnev was still in power and there were hundreds of men and women still in prison for their Christian activities.

More recently the historian Vadim Chubinsky reviewed a novel, *The Scaffold*, by the popular Central Asian writer, Chingiz Aitmatov, and commented on his choice of a Christian believer as his main character:

> A significant (and strangely enough, not diminishing) section of the Soviet population – Christians and Muslims – believe in God, and a smaller section, also not insignificant in numbers, belong to the various cults. These people live and work alongside us, think and suffer and search for the meaning of life, argue amongst themselves; and even those of them who are professional 'churchmen' increasingly co-operate with us – for instance, in the peace movement. So is it right for them to be banished from our literature? Common sense replies – no; the very nature of the mission of literature says – no. Now Aitmatov has boldly broken into this virgin soil in literature; this first attempt may be imperfect in some ways, but surely it is worthy of recognition?[8]

Some *samizdat* authors of the Khrushchev–Brezhnev period much more openly embrace Christianity. Andrei Sinyavsky, now in exile in Paris, is an Orthodox believer. Nadezhda Mandelstam's biography of her late husband movingly recounts the role the faith played in their brief life together. The passionate Christian poetry of Irina Ratushinskaya, who belongs to the generation born in the 1950s, did not come out of a vacuum, but continues a tradition from the days of Tolstoy and Dostoevsky which was never completely ruptured.

In the world of art and music dozens of artists have expressed their faith in one way or another. The cellist Mstislav Rostropovich has shown that his dedication to music is grounded firmly in his allegiance to the faith of the Russian Orthodox Church. Among composers of the present day, Edison Denisov, Sofia Gubaidulina, and especially Alfred Schnittke, have expressed religious influences in their work, while Christian idealism so dominated the thinking of the Estonian, Arvo Pärt, that he had to emigrate to evade discrimination and unofficial banning of his compositions.

Religious themes are no less evident in the Soviet cinema. Naturally, these were usually implied rather than explicit, in order to stand some chance (not always successful) of circumventing the censor, more active here than in the field of literature, because a popular film would make a much more widespread impact.

Andrei Tarkovsky (1932–86) was brought up by his divorced mother in a Christian atmosphere, even though Stalin's terror reigned outside the house. The author of a recent perceptive study of his work writes:

> While it is doubtful that Tarkovsky gained much of an understanding of the liturgical life of the Orthodox Church or of its theology – books on theology, including the writings of the Church Fathers, would have been unavailable, though Tarkovsky was able to read the Bible – he seems to have been raised in an attitude of sympathy towards a church which was being harshly persecuted, indeed almost annihilated, during his boyhood . . . The art of Andrei Tarkovsky . . . points simultaneously toward the Orthodox Christian 'millennium' of Russian history and toward the dark pagan enchantment from which Vladimir of Kiev extracted the country in the tenth century.[9]

Tarkovsky's films were ambiguous and their dense imagery made them difficult to understand at first, but the censors, who waged a constant, but ultimately unsuccessful, battle with him, realised that here was a major figure dealing with man's central spiritual concerns in a totally non-communist way. *Andrei Rublyov* (1969) is one of the most complex historical films ever made, in which Tarkovsky attempts to recreate the religious and artistic atmosphere of the late fourteenth and early fifteenth centuries in a completely authentic and unprettified way. *Solaris* (1972) brings the themes of conscience and atonement into the unexpected context of science fiction. *The Mirror* and *Stalker*, both intricate films full of imagery containing both Christian and pagan elements, were made only under the greatest difficulties. Eventually Tarkovsky emigrated in 1984 and openly declared his Orthodox faith, while making his last two films in exile. He died of cancer in 1986 at the age of fifty-four, without experiencing the fruits of *perestroika*, the acceptance of his films in the Soviet Union, or the opportunity to return to his native land, as other artists in conflict, such as Rostropovich, Ashkenazy the pianist, and Lyubimov, the theatrical producer, were able to do.

Tengiz Abuladze's anti-Stalinist film, *Repentance*, took Moscow by storm when it was released in 1987. It tells the story of an artist, Sandro Baratelli, who is persecuted by the despotic Varlam, the mayor of a small Georgian town. The two characters come into conflict over a church which Varlam has turned into a science laboratory; Baratelli wants to preserve it as an essential part of the town's cultural and spiritual heritage. The church is later destroyed. For any Soviet citizen, the film is evocative of the Stalinist era, with the subsequent arrest and disappearance of Baratelli and the persecution of his relatives. The common theme of 'artist as prophet' or truth seeker, which crops up often in Russian literature, is here used to point to the need for repentance, the central idea of the film. The last scenes show an elderly lady asking Baratelli's daughter if the street she is on leads to the church. 'This street is named after Varlam: it cannot lead to the church.' 'What use is it if it does not lead to the church?' is the poignant reply, the last words of the film.

Religion has begun to play a prominent part in documentary films as well. For example, in 1988 during the celebration of the Millennium of Christianity cinemas all over the country were showing the highly artistic and beautiful study of the spiritual life of the Orthodox Church, *Khram* ('Church'), and it was also screened on television.

More recently there has been an amazing documentary, showing how the great monastic complex on the Solovki Islands in the White Sea was converted into one of Lenin's first prison camps. The film interviewed former inmates and included extracts from a Soviet prison documentary made before such enterprises became impossible.

The key moment for the emergence of public debate on the re-instatement of Christian values was 10 December 1986, when the youth newspaper, *Komsomolskaya pravda*, printed two opposing views on the value of religion in cultural life. A conservative critic, Kryvelyov, had earlier attacked the religious and mystical leanings of such writers as Chingiz Aitmatov and Viktor Astafiev, who were 'flirting with the gods'.

The reply came from Yevgeni Yevtushenko, angry young poet of the 1960s, who had become a kind of 'official dissident', often sent abroad to help the regime to prove how 'tolerant' it was. He was often under fire from those suffering for their non-conformist views. From this time on, however, Yevtushenko became a spokesman for the Gorbachev reforms. He stated that it was a weakness of Soviet culture that it felt obliged to put on counter-attractions at Easter to entice young people away from something genuinely beautiful, the ageless rituals of the Orthodox Church in their finest expression. 'The countenances of saints,' he wrote, 'painted by geniuses of the people, have more popular appeal than the stony frozen faces of those on boards of honour' (this is a reference to the Soviet practice of depicting heroes of labour and other such characters on notice boards outside the public enterprises where they work).

Throughout history, Yevtushenko continued, religion has at times played a positive role, which is not to deny that its influence has also sometimes been negative – but surely an objective assessment should now be possible? The Bible was a book which, in cultural terms, had immense value:

> I cannot understand why state presses have printed the Koran and not the Bible. Without Biblical knowledge young people are unable to understand much of Pushkin, Gogol, Dostoevsky and Tolstoy. The early Mayakovsky is full of Biblical imagery. The Bible fetches a huge sum in second-hand bookshops and on the black market. If Kryvelyov wants everybody to become convinced atheists, how can they be without a knowledge of the Bible? 'Forbidden fruit is sweet.' The socialist world-view cannot exist in a vacuum: you cannot adopt a theory without measuring it against other theories . . . Atheism in and of itself is not a source of morality; the source of morality is culture – culture in terms of human behaviour, conscience, knowledge of what is true and what is false . . . The source of morality is, in fact, life itself, people, creativity. Total unbelief is worse than false belief. There are universal, immutable values based on the struggle of humanity for justice.[10]

Published alongside his article is a rebuttal by a philosopher, Suren Kaltakhchian, who quoted Lenin's argument that the only true culture was one which furthered the development of society – and religion did not: 'Religion did not enrich culture, but extracted everything possible from it that could be used to increase its own influence.' It was necessary, he concluded, to stick to Marxist-Leninist ideology at all costs, as this teaching was all-sufficient for an understanding of the world.

This debate has developed in various ways. For example, Andrei Nuikin wrote in the influential literary journal *Novy mir* ('New World') in April 1987 that it was a poor kind of atheism which rejected religion out of hand or tackled it in a superficial or biased way. He fiercely attacked the kind of mindless hard-line dogmatism which was still finding a home in the Soviet press and contended that it was essential for any writer who tackled religion to be well versed in the subject.

True atheism must have a sound philosophical basis and unless mature creative thinking was encouraged and crude indoctrination avoided, Soviet society would produce not atheists, but 'mere godless men'.[11]

This argument seems now to have gained the upper hand since the Millennium celebrations of June 1988. Atheism in the Soviet media is clearly beating a fast retreat. In March 1989 a letter appeared in *Sovetskaya kultura* ('Soviet Culture') from a 'convinced atheist', who lamented the moral state of society, which was now manifesting all the social evils attributed for so long to its bourgeois equivalent. It was difficult to live without faith. Atheists believed in man, his high moral qualities and potential, in the attainment of communism – but what now? Religion had its own system of beliefs and offered a key to the human soul. The more churches were destroyed, the more the positive values relative to them disappeared. Now the time was past for communism to be afraid of religion and to treat believers as ignorant and fanatical. The Bible should be as easy to obtain as an ideological pamphlet and society would gain immeasurably from this.[12]

Even the main newspapers, such as *Izvestia*, reflected such a view. Two women wrote a letter published in the same month as the above:

> So many times we have heard our grandmothers' stories about their youth. We have been struck by the culture prevalent in those times . . . And now? Now we are persecuted by sex. Time and again we hear: prostitution! A normal, decent girl is simply afraid to go outdoors in the evening. Many people now think that truly pure and unclouded love has died . . . Why all this? It's because we have gone away from religion.[13]

The Christian Academician, Dimitri Sergeyevich Likhachev, talked at length to a correspondent of the magazine *Semya* ('Family') in the summer of 1988 on the essential contribution of Russian Orthodoxy to the whole origin of national culture.[14]

The overall impact of the rehabilitation of Christian and spiritual themes in every aspect of the media is penetrating to the general public. People are rapidly regaining part of their heritage which they believed they had lost for ever. Of course, the ban on religion over three generations, combined with the enforced atheist teaching at all levels from kindergarten to university, has left an immense void which it will take much more than a few novels and films to fill. The limitless hunger for the spiritual is a fact of life for tens of millions of people, but it is unfocused and undirected. Uncontrolled access to the media of proponents of any and every philosophy and paranormal experimentation holds out its own peculiar set of dangers which will need to be tackled in some concerted way.

One disturbing instance illustrating this very point was the televising of faith-healing sessions by A. Kashpirovsky in the autumn of 1989. He has gained a considerable reputation in the Soviet Union for his powers of hypnosis. These sessions were televised as part of a new slot in Sunday television: there is now a Sunday Moral Sermon, where church leaders such as Metropolitan Pitirim have give fifteen-minute talks; on other Sundays the programme has been devoted to Kashpirovsky's healing sessions which were over an hour long. These caused great controversy in the USSR and were the subject of a full page spread in the weekly newspaper *Literaturnaya gazeta* in December. Academic specialists asked if Kashpirovsky was a latter-day Rasputin with a similar corrupting influence in society. The paper also printed an extract from the *Journal of the Moscow Patriarchate* which briefly outlined Christian teaching on exorcism and the occult. The sessions are no longer televised, but the incident merely serves to illustrate how easily people who have been deprived of spiritual food for so long can be led into practices that are incompatible with church teaching.

'The Rehabilitation of Christian Ethical Values in the Soviet Media', as Dr William van den Bercken, of Utrecht University, calls a recent study of religious *glasnost* in the media, is one of the most significant and profound changes of the Gorbachev era, one which most of our radio and newspaper correspondents have lost sight of amid the welter of daily developments in the political field. He notes evidence of this everywhere and concludes:

> To Soviet man the problem of Stalinism and the Brezhnev-lie transcends party politics and historiography. Neither legal rehabilitation of the victims nor revision of history will be enough to overcome the legacy of the past. The Soviet Union under Gorbachev is undergoing a basic change of mentality. The significance of traditional Christian values in this reassessment process is that they arise not out of church involvement, but out of the independent search by Soviet intellectuals for ethical guarantees against the past repeating itself.[15]

The Christian Gospel, in the age of Mr Gorbachev's *glasnost*, is now reflected in the Soviet media in a way which, considering the previous seventy years of Soviet atheism, is little less than miraculous. The policies instituted by Gorbachev, as we shall see, have had a special role to play in the development of the life of the churches in the USSR over the past two to three years. Events such as his accession to power in March 1985 and the Orthodox Millennium three years later will surely go down in history as key factors in the turning of the tide for religious liberty.

2 Gorbachev and His Times

A New Man for New Times

In Rome, 1978 became known as the 'year of the three Popes'. The election and sudden death of yet another Italian Pope (John Paul I) seemed to many a divine intervention conveying the strongest possible message that it was time for a complete change of direction. The conclave of Cardinals looked to where the church was strongest and elected a Pole.

Soon afterwards, the Soviet Union saw a similar process. The time-lapse was a little longer – Brezhnev died on 10 November 1982; Gorbachev was elected on 11 March 1985 – but it included no fewer than three deaths and four leaders. History will judge whether or not divine intervention operated in the Kremlin: Andropov was soon seen to be deteriorating physically; the election of the obviously ailing Chernenko to succeed him was a stop-gap measure. The Presidium was left no alternative but to choose a man young enough to withstand the physical demands of the job and flexible enough to overhaul the complicated and archaic system with decisive and innovative policies.

Nearly twenty years under Brezhnev had led the Soviet Union to the brink of economic catastrophe. But the successive appointment of two men who were visibly – and in the case of Chernenko, frequently and embarrassingly before the eyes of the world on television – unable to perform even the simplest offices of state must also have had a psychological effect on the Soviet people. Andropov, to be sure, had a decisive personality, as one would expect of a man who had risen through the toughest of systems to become head of the state security (KGB), but he was sixty-eight years old on his appointment and it rapidly became obvious that his best years were behind him. The world's press, with more optimism than soundness of judgment, dubbed him an 'intellectual' and an 'innovator', but his plans did not amount to much more than a drive against corruption, and even this was cut short by his ill health. One noteworthy action was his promotion of Gorbachev within the Politburo – indeed some commentators believe that it was he who paved the way for Gorbachev's reforms. Chernenko, who could scarcely speak, achieved nothing of note.

By this time there was a generation of young people who could not remember even the era of Khrushchev's reforms, which had ended twenty years before. For a long time most citizens accepted the threat of foreign invasion as a justification for the massive military build-up, without recognising that this was a major factor in the general economic deprivation. Most sharply of all, the gradual penetration of images from the West, through foreign broadcasts and contacts with visitors, began to prove that beyond those impassable frontiers there was a different mode of existence where people did not live six to a room. The facts of underdeveloped Soviet economic life were not the only realities in the world. Change was long overdue; a leader of vigour and vision was needed.

Mikhail Sergeyevich Gorbachev was born in 1931 in the remote village of Privolnoye, Stavropol Region, in the south of Russia. He needed physical endurance even to survive to the point where his mental toughness could begin to set him on his way towards a special career.[1] Of the millions who died in the famines in the Ukraine and southern Russia during the 1930s, possibly as many as 30,000 came from his own region. When he was eleven, the invading Nazi army penetrated just far enough east to occupy his home village and this hostile influx must have had a profound influence on him. Nearly fifty years later, however, this would not prevent him from tacitly approving the reforms occurring in the German Democratic Republic; his policy of non-intervention over the destruction of the Berlin Wall being a decisive factor in the rush towards democracy in Eastern Europe.

Many neighbouring families suffered far worse than the Gorbachevs, not only from the famine, but from the enforced collectivisation. Gorbachev's grandfather was not a dispossessed land-owner, but a peasant who benefited from the new system to become director of the local collective farm. After the war he played a key role in rebuilding the economy of the area. His father, wounded on the Polish front in the war, became a tractor driver on the *kolkhoz*. He died in 1976.

It was a normal enough background for a boy growing up in the Soviet Union in the 1930s. There was nothing unusual, either, in having a parent or a grandparent who was a believer. Gorbachev's mother was a practising Orthodox Christian and he was baptised. She still lives in the same village and, apparently, is a believer to this day. The young Mikhail probably went to church and would have heard from his mother at an early age, well before starting school, something of the persecution of religion during these times of great hardship.

His early education at the local primary school, later at secondary school, then finally at Moscow State University (1950–55), included not only the standard lessons on Marxism-Leninism, but a compulsory course on 'scientific atheism'. A pass was necessary in this for acceptance at any university, not least Moscow, which attracted the intellectual elite of the Soviet Union, but which was barred to all but the most ideologically reliable.

It seems likely that the enforced dogma predominated over the 'vestiges of the past' (to use the standard phrase of the propaganda of the time) which Gorbachev would have experienced at his mother's knee. This was in contrast to many other families, where children sincerely wanting to be Christians were thrown into constant conflict with teachers at school.

Gorbachev was in Moscow as a law student when Stalin died in 1953. The nation was psychologically unprepared for this event and many feared for the future. Only a few could see that a new age was dawning, offering openings within the system for young people with ambition. A certain subdued anticipation of the future may have tempered the grief Gorbachev shared with his fellow-students, including Raisa Maximovna, whom he met and married during his student years. Without the necessary contacts in Moscow, he was unable to get a job in the capital on completion of his degree and was forced to return to Stavropol to begin an arduous climb up the Party ladder.

Gorbachev's law degree from Moscow University gave him local status, even at an early age. As a dedicated Party man, he was not afraid to criticise, but first of all he always observed. He began to take note of the many defects in the system. Given his background, he was particularly interested in agriculture. He saw it falling massively short of its potential, even in an area of high production like his own, where good soil and a warmer climate gave it an advantage over the harsher north. He must have asked himself whether collectivisation could ever provide the plenty it was supposed to do. Mechanisation simply failed to happen according to the five-year plans. Even where there were tractors, spare parts were woefully short, often keeping the machines out of the fields for weeks at a time. Here, as in many branches of industry, a kind of barter system grew up, in which only material inducements could be sure of making the wheels of production turn. It was only a short step from this to the corruption which was to become endemic.

He saw the toll of days lost to drunkenness, so that when he was finally in a position of supreme authority one of his first edicts curbed the massive sale of alcohol and banned it from Kremlin functions – a brave attempt at reform which failed through popular resistance and complaints at the loss of income from the taxes.

In the meantime, Raisa worked on her doctoral thesis, entitled 'The Emergence of New Characteristics in the Daily Lives of the Collective Farm Peasantry'[2], which was based on sociological investigations in the region. In many respects this was a pioneering work, which undoubtedly had an influence on her husband's later reform programme.

Gorbachev became Stavropol First Secretary at the age of thirty-nine. He was an energetic and popular Party chief with a reputation for getting results. He also had the advantage of presiding over an area of spa towns patronised by members of the Kremlin leadership: it was at the town of Kislovodsk that he first met Andropov and was able assiduously to cultivate good relations with the future General Secretary, himself from the Stavropol region. Gorbachev followed in the footsteps of another ambitious Party man, Kulakov, who had been responsible for Gorbachev's appointment as Party chief following his own promotion to Moscow. Suslov, the chief Party ideologist, also a former Stavropol Party First Secretary, is similarly believed to have promoted Gorbachev. Thus it was that Gorbachev found himself back in Moscow, promoted to the position of Secretary of the Central Committee responsible for agriculture in December 1978.[3]

Gorbachev in Moscow

In 1980 Gorbachev was promoted to be a full member of the Politburo, although he was still virtually unknown to the world at large. He made his mark quickly, travelling abroad energetically and impressing those he met. On his first visit to Britain he met Mrs Thatcher, establishing a good relationship on which he was later to build. It was she who coined the phrase that Gorbachev was a 'man you can do business with'.

On his election as General Secretary of the Communist Party of the Soviet Union on 11 March 1985, Gorbachev appeared as a figure who had spent most of his life in the provinces, far away from the intrigues of the Kremlin and apparently uncorrupted by them. During his first months in office, he showed himself to be his own man, ready to take decisive action particularly in restructuring the top of the *apparat* around him, but in no sense stepping beyond the boundaries within which any good Marxist-Leninist could have been expected to move. He must, however, have been deeply troubled to realise the full depth of the economic crisis which he had inherited and the massive commitment he faced in the arms race, which deflected into sterile confrontation untold billions of roubles which were sorely needed for economic development. He had also inherited international opprobrium for his country's invasion of Afghanistan six years earlier, whilst thousands of grieving families believed they had lost their sons to a useless cause. Led by a well-organised Jewish lobby, world criticism confronted him with the shameful Soviet human rights record of recent years.

In the autumn of 1985 Gorbachev visited France. In an interview for French television broadcast on 30 September, he showed his willingness to debate human rights issues, but without making any dramatic departure from established policies:

> Let us in the Soviet Union manage our own affairs . . . The question of human rights presents no difficulties for us. We are prepared to debate this question anywhere . . . Of course, we have people who follow their own logic, clash with Soviet power and with socialism and profess a different ideology. Problems arise here in those cases in which an individual comes into conflict with the law. That was what happened to Shcharansky . . . When questions of the reunification of families arise, we agree to this, except in cases where people know state secrets.[4]

Four months later, again addressing a French public, but this time through the communist newspaper, *L'Humanité*, Gorbachev stated:

> Soviet Jewry have become the cause of psychological warfare waged against the USSR . . . I believe that in a civilised society there must be no room at all for anti-semitism, Zionism or any other manifestations of nationalism, chauvinism or racism. Now for political prisoners. We have none, just as we do not persecute people for their convictions. But any state must protect itself against those who try to subvert it.[5]

It was obviously extremely difficult then for Gorbachev to take more than a single step at a time. One can discern an attempt to placate the old guard in his painful repetition of tarnished propaganda in the immediate continuation of the interview in *L'Humanité* quoted above: 'Now Sakharov. Measures were taken regarding him in accordance with our legislation . . . Sakharov lives in Gorky in normal conditions, conducts research and remains an Academician. He is in normal health, as far as I know.'

Within three days Anatoli Shcharansky walked free. He was one of the outstanding Soviet human rights activists, whose marriage to Avital and her long years of campaigning during his subsequent imprisonment turned him into one of the world's best-known political detainees. On 11 February 1986 his diminutive figure, striding alone across the Glienicke Bridge between East and West Berlin, hands holding up trousers many sizes too big for him, was an unmistakable signal that something new was happening in the Soviet Union. A factor in this must have been the continual demonstrations suffered by any Soviet statesman making a foray outside the Eastern bloc. But here already were the first stirrings of desire to establish what Mr Gorbachev was later to call a 'law-governed state'.

Between the release of Shcharansky and the Reykjavik summit in the autumn of 1986 an event occurred which shook Gorbachev and all the Kremlin leaders to the core: Chernobyl. The week-long silence of the leadership following the explosion at the nuclear reactor indicates the magnitude of the shock. There was a clear policy break at this point. Everyone could see that the system was totally unprepared to deal with any major crisis; basic improvements were imperative. The pace of change began to accelerate. Chernobyl is in Ukraine and some saw that republic as a victim of Moscow's policies. Demands began to be heard that the republics should have greater control over their own affairs. Now opposition to environmental pollution, which not so long ago had been treated as virtually treasonable, was gaining momentum. The Chernobyl disaster put huge areas of good agricultural land out of production and therefore placed an immense strain on already overstretched economic resources. Internationally, this was the moment at which it became evident that atomic energy, whether for offensive or peaceful uses, was not a panacea for mankind; the stage was set for the first offer of wide-ranging concessions in the armaments race.

By the time of the Reykjavik summit, begun at short notice and with little preparation less than six months after Chernobyl, on 10 October 1986, it was obvious that Mr Gorbachev was determined to present a new face to President Reagan and to the world. In the few hours of hiatus between the departure of the leaders from their capitals and the opening of the conference itself the world received dramatic news. It could not have come at a more advantageous time, with the media anxious to report on something substantial from inside the Soviet Union.

One of the most notorious unresolved human rights cases was the imprisonment and treatment of the young poet Irina Ratushinskaya. Her 'crime' had been to write poetry of a personal and Christian nature, containing clear elements of protest against oppression; for this she had been sentenced as recently as 1983, at the age of twenty-eight, to seven years' imprisonment in a strict regime labour camp followed by five years of exile. Keston College had passed on to the world urgent messages about her deteriorating health, along with new poems smuggled out of the prison. Dick Rodgers, an Anglican minister who had spearheaded a number of campaigns for religious liberty in the Soviet Union, spent the whole of Lent 1986 in a cage in his home city of Birmingham subjecting himself to conditions and a diet which as nearly as possible reproduced those Irina was simultaneously undergoing. His initiative may well have saved her life.

Early on the morning the summit was due to begin, Keston College received a telephone call from Irina herself, back in her home city of Kiev, announcing that she had been released unconditionally the previous day and was now expecting to emigrate with her husband. For a few hours this became the lead story in the world's press.

It would be easy to describe this move as a cynical attempt by Mr Gorbachev to win a major propaganda victory and seize an unexpected advantage at a key time. His move certainly won him the credit he sought, but it turned out to be no mere ploy to gain favour, for it paved the way for another dramatic move, which turned out to be much more than a gesture. Two months later Gorbachev telephoned Academician Andrei Sakharov in exile in the city of Gorky, whither Brezhnev had sent him with no pretence of a trial. Gorky was closed to foreigners, so the aim had been to sever his overseas contacts, but his wife, Yelena Bonner, by coming periodically to Moscow, had managed nevertheless to keep some lines of communication open. As he was by far the best-known democratic reformer in the USSR, his recall to Moscow sent to the Soviet people and to the world the strongest possible signal that there were to be far-reaching changes in the ordering of society. There were some who believed Sakharov was by now a broken man who had compromised himself.

Gorbachev can scarcely have envisaged that just two years later Sakharov would be elected to the new Congress of People's Deputies, that its debates would rivet the nation to its TV sets and that one of the most memorable transmitted images would be the elected deputy, Sakharov, challenging him face to face over the Communist Party's right to supremacy. Gorbachev's evident grief at the sudden death of Sakharov just after this on 14 December 1989 illustrates the respect he undoubtedly feels for intellectuals, even those who do not share his beliefs, such as another deputy, Academician Dimitri Likhachev (not to be confused with the conservative politician Ligachev), an outstanding layman of the Russian Orthodox Church. Indeed, it is true to say that, unlike his predecessors, Gorbachev is himself one of the intelligentsia, as is his wife.

Sakharov's return inaugurated the process, which lasted right through the next year, of releasing nearly all the four hundred or so religious prisoners and the much larger number of political detainees.

However, the Soviet human rights record was not always displaying such positive signs at this stage. Barely three weeks before Sakharov's return from exile – and perhaps also influencing Gorbachev's decision – another veteran Soviet human rights campaigner, Anatoli Marchenko, died in the notorious Chistopol prison. He had spent twenty of his forty-eight years in Soviet prison camps. Arrested originally on charges of alleged hooliganism after a brawl, he discovered the full brutality of the Soviet penal system. His observations evolved into a book, *My Testimony*, which circulated in *samizdat* and was published in the West in 1968. He was serving a fifteen-year sentence for anti-Soviet agitation and propaganda when he died as a result of KGB brutality.

The Jewish community continued, with considerable justification, to complain that the emigration laws had not been relaxed to the extent needed to clear the huge backlog of people waiting to leave the Soviet Union. But the reception Mr Gorbachev subsequently received in Washington and Bonn showed him that at least one aspect of his policy had succeeded, for rarely has a visiting foreign statesman received such an ecstatic welcome in either city.

While these events were taking place, the thankless grind of trying to activate the economy was beginning. The world embraced *glasnost* and *perestroika*, which became household words. The first is usually translated as 'openness', but its root is *golos* (voice) and long before this the word had existed in a human rights context with the connotation of 'giving voice (or publicity)' to injustice. It was an emotive concept and it became the watchword of a new age. Gorbachev probably thinks of *perestroika* ('restructuring') as more important; scarcely a day passes without his criticising those who resist it. At times he seems to try to give it a persona of its own, but one can sense his frustration as he fails to find enough people at middle or lower levels able and willing to implement the vision he proclaims from above. Everywhere now in Soviet society one sees *glasnost* in abundance, so much so that some are growing tired of the superabundance of information previously shrouded from view. By contrast, the progress of *perestroika* is negligible in the very economic sphere into which Gorbachev launched it. In some areas, however, especially the arts, religion and now nationalism, *perestroika* has moved ahead with shattering speed – so much so that the political map of Europe had to be torn up and replaced by a new one in the three months between October and December 1989. Another of Mr Gorbachev's key concepts, *demokratizatsia*, played a major role here.

There was a clear distinction in Gorbachev's mind between 'democratisation' and 'democracy'. The former represented a process designed to galvanise the supine political processes into activity and provide some real leadership in the republics. The latter, under the scrutiny of even the most elementary logic, would mean the disintegration of the Soviet system. This is indeed happening, but he certainly did not intend to precipitate it. *Demokratizatsia* was intended to be some kind of halfway house, a limbo in which the Communist Party could always blow the whistle and remind the contestants of the ground rules. The concept was not a sham, as demonstrated by the setting up of elections to the new Congress of People's Deputies at the end of March 1989. The process was controlled from the top to produce the inevitable communist majority, but the process had invigorated some Party members, such as Yuri Afanasiev and Boris Yeltsin, who led a most outspoken campaign of dissent. There were also genuine lists of non-Party candidates, many of whom were successful in the first legal exercise of the democratic right since 1917. The effect was to produce an enormous burst of self-confidence in the satellite countries of Eastern Europe, and the certainty in the Baltic States that the course on which they were already embarked was not a romantic one leading inevitably to disaster, but a realistic one, in which the statesmanlike approach which they were already so notably demonstrating had a serious chance of achieving the independence they had lost fifty years earlier. The first fragment of masonry from the Berlin Wall in the hand of a demonstrator whose action went unpunished was proof to every nationalist and democrat, and even to millions who had not dared to think that way before, that resolute action could now sound the death-knell of a massive system of oppression and overthrow Soviet communism once and for all.

Opposition to Gorbachev

The advent of *glasnost* has illuminated the secret deliberations of the Kremlin leadership hardly at all (though even in a democracy such as Britain Cabinet discussions cannot come into the public domain for thirty years after they have taken place). Therefore we know little about the real nature of the opposition to Mr Gorbachev at this time. No explanation is yet forthcoming as to why the Red Army stood by in apparent impotence while the basic prop of their policy, the Warsaw Pact, disintegrated in the three months between October and Christmas 1989; or why the KGB acquiesced as central control over the republics collapsed and the whole Soviet system appeared to be tottering towards a rapid end. The old logic would have demanded the hardening of opposition and the overthrow of Gorbachev at a dozen different points, but he has shown statesmanship of unprecedented calibre in dominating the public debates, staying one jump ahead of his opponents and even turning to his advantage the endless contradictions, where what he has dismissed as impossible one week is implemented the next.

In these astonishing days extraordinary explanations abound of how these events have taken such a course. Before we come to our central discussion of the effect all this would have on religious life, perhaps it is worth quoting the most exotic theory on offer: even this is not entirely without credibility. It goes something like this.

In the developing arms race and with the stagnant Soviet economy, disaster seemed to be looming ever closer. Soviet military might could maintain its lead only by draining more and more from the economy, but this could not move forward because of the huge gap between Soviet and American technology. Far from 'overtaking America' (the watchword of the Khrushchev era), the Soviet Union was destined to fall further and further behind. In the USA the simplest processes were computerised, while the Soviet Union kept its insufficient photocopiers under lock and key. That disparity was growing daily and the Soviet Union was degenerating to the economic status of a third-world country. The 'Star Wars' programme of President Reagan gave the uncomfortable feeling that this technology gap would before long annihilate even the capability of the Soviets to deliver a nuclear strike beyond their own territory. The refined espionage techniques of the KGB, especially in the industrial sphere, were producing the message that current Soviet development had reached an impasse; only the most dramatic solution could now offer any hope.

Someone trustworthy and decisive had to be found who would lead the Soviet Union along a new path. It was the KGB, it is argued, who held the real power in the Soviet Union; they discovered Gorbachev virtually within their own ranks, a protégé of their former head, Yuri Andropov, to whom he owed his rapid rise to the Politburo. Therefore, according to this theory, Gorbachev owes the apparent unassailability of his position to the direct protection of the KGB, which gave him *carte blanche* to implement a dramatic programme, though doubtless without their seeing that the logical end of that road would be the disintegration of the system.

A counter-argument to this is the fact that Chebrikov, head of the KGB on Gorbachev's accession, apparently turned against him when his programme became more radical, but the highest Party organs were strong enough, first to move him sideways, then to retire him.

That there was still considerable opposition along the way, even if this theory should prove correct, is demonstrated by the occasional rallies of the counter forces. A non-democratic leader is always particularly vulnerable while absent abroad, as Mr Ceausescu found to his cost during his visit to Iran in December 1989. While Mr Gorbachev was absent in Cuba and then in London in April 1989 there were two separate assaults on his authority. The first was the sending-in of the troops to quell a peaceful nationalist demonstration in Tbilisi, Georgia, with the subsequent massacre, an action which Gorbachev could never have sanctioned. The second was a legal event which was quite out of keeping with his policy before and since.

On the very day after his return to Moscow from London – a Saturday, incidentally – Gorbachev signed a decree which seemed to negate some of the very advances he had been fighting for over the past three years. It consisted of amendments to the old law on crimes against the state, under which so many people had been imprisoned over the last thirty years. It proclaimed a punishment of between three and ten years for acquiring 'material assets or technical means from organisations abroad or their representatives' for 'undermining the political and economic system of the USSR'.[6] Such catch-all phrases threatened all who had contact with foreigners, warning them against receiving even such essential items as photocopying machines. While the decree did not specifically mention religious believers, these groups felt seriously at risk, because often in the past the demand for religious reform had been quoted in the courts as an act prejudicial to the state. The decree went on to designate a three-year sentence for those who called for 'betrayal of the homeland'. Which homeland? Clearly, the decree meant the 'Soviet homeland', but this was at a time when the very concept was disintegrating and nationalist movements in Georgia and the Baltic States were already operating openly.

The only other signature on the document beside Gorbachev's was that of the Georgian, T. Menteshashvili, Secretary of the Presidium of the Supreme Soviet (Gorbachev was its chairman). The only plausible explanation for such a blow against *perestroika* is that a group of hard-liners must have used the Georgian demonstration as the cue for saying 'enough is enough', put the document together in haste and presented Gorbachev with a 'sign or else' ultimatum virtually as he stepped off the aeroplane. A further spur to action must have been the elections to the new Congress of People's Deputies just a week earlier, as a result of which a number of the old guard received their marching orders. Ironically, it was precisely this body which was now designated to see through any new legislation, and here was its authority undermined before it had even met. The end of this episode was nevertheless a victory for Gorbachev's real plans: when the new body did meet, it repealed the act, which had never reached the stage of implementation.

Human Rights

Whatever forces prevail, there can be no doubt that, in general terms, Mr Gorbachev set out to safeguard human rights in the new society he wished to build. A concrete sign of this was the setting up at the end of 1987 of a 'Public Commission for Humanitarian Questions and Human Rights', known as the Burlatsky Commission, after its chairman. This was a direct response to worldwide criticisms of the Soviet record on human rights.

Fyodor Burlatsky himself is a man to note. In *Literaturnaya gazeta* on 1 October 1986 he opened the door to a major debate on human rights by publishing an article in which he constructed an imaginary dialogue between an opponent and a supporter of *perestroika*. The opponent says it will all come to nothing, just as happened in the period after Stalin. The advocate claims that this time it will be different, for now there is sufficient 'political will and courage'. In an interview which he gave to an American Christian journalist in September 1988, he talks of his career to date:

> I was educated in law. During the late 1950s I tried to push for the creation of political science as an academic discipline. I was interested in the relationship between the state, democracy and human rights. For example, in 1957 I published an article about the process of democratization after the Twentieth Party Congress, which included human rights problems. I practised law for about three years, then I became a journalist . . . I was chairman of the so-called 'scientific' political advisory group during the Khrushchev era, and was his speech-writer. After he was purged, I returned to my scientific and journalistic activities. Then, at the beginning of the Gorbachev era, I realized that there were new possibilities for activities with some progressive and 'radical' intellectuals. It was my idea to create this commission on human rights.[7]

Mr Burlatsky backed up his words with his deeds as soon as his Commission was in place. He proved that this would not be mainly a propaganda exercise by calling for the release of Soviet political and religious prisoners, entering into well-publicised negotiations with a group set up by Mrs Rosalyn Carter, wife of the former American President, about individual names remaining on the list of detainees. He also promoted the legalisation of the Ukrainian Catholic Church, in the interview quoted above, more than a year before this came about, and criticised Soviet bureaucracy in 1989 when many of the projected new laws seemed to be disappearing into limbo between the promise and the drafting.

The Burlatsky Commission moved ahead of international agreements, but in the spirit of the negotiations going on at the time. During 1988 a lengthy conference in Vienna reviewed and reformulated the Helsinki Accords of 1975. Here, for the first time, the subject of human rights was singled out as demanding its own special series of conferences. Press freedom, the right to emigrate and environmental issues received similar attention from the thirty-five original signatories to the 1975 agreement (all the countries of Europe except Albania, plus the USA and Canada). Given the tensions between Eastern and Western Europe at the time, it was a triumph of patient diplomacy that all these signatories, who fourteen years earlier had been concerned mainly with security and the guaranteeing of existing borders, should now be prepared to sharpen the focus and agree to a systematic examination of human rights abuses and restrictions on religious liberty over the whole of their diffuse territory.   ·

The holding of a human rights conference in Moscow had now

become official Soviet policy, since Gorbachev had requested it, virtually off the cuff, at the Reykjavik summit. Some observers interpreted the establishment of the Burlatsky Commission as deliberately preparing the way for this goal; others saw in it an attempt to short-circuit the activities of the various rival independent human rights groups which were now proliferating in Moscow and other cities.

With the conclusion of the Vienna conference in January 1989, the Soviets did indeed secure assent to their conference proposal, but only as the culmination of a series of three meetings to be held in Paris in June 1989, Copenhagen a year later and Moscow in October 1991. The British Government made it clear that it would attend the final one only if there were a significant improvement in Soviet human rights performance, not least in the area of religious liberty; the preceding two conferences would monitor carefully the progress of the Soviet Union and the other countries of the Eastern bloc. As one of the six official British delegates to the Paris conference, three from the Foreign and Commonwealth Office, three from independent monitoring groups known as NGOs (Non-Governmental Organisations), I was able to observe for myself that the process began in a satisfactory way. Though the discussions were so formal as to preclude any cut-and-thrust debate, delegates raised and therefore put on record all the major issues. Representatives from Eastern Europe, not least Romania, were prepared to listen to detailed accounts of their shortcomings. In the past, sharp criticisms of individual nations in various international forums have sometimes led to a walk-out, but there was no suggestion of this in the Paris meeting.

From now on, then, the governments of Western Europe and North America (but the Soviet Government, too, in the shape of the Burlatsky Commission) were prepared to set up modest departments and to put money into the promotion of human rights, a very real contribution to the development of international law and one which must set a standard for other troubled areas of the world.

Whatever the outcome of the series of conferences in a 'Helsinki area' vastly different from the one in which the original agreements were signed, the interim conclusion must be that the Soviet authorities were taking their commitment to human rights seriously at a time when the central authority of a Kremlin directive still meant something. Although the political upheavals of 1990 have meant that the Burlatsky Commission now receives less attention than formerly, it is still an important symbol as a pressure group during Gorbachev's struggle to achieve a law-governed society.

Religious Liberty

From the time of Mr Gorbachev's accession in 1985, it became probable that there would be a softer line on religion, though no one could have foreseen the dramatic initiatives that the new leader would take three years later. During the first six months the press was virtually silent on religion, with the exception of a conventional article in *Pravda* on 13 September 1985. Just over a month later the draft of the new Communist Party programme appeared in the same newspaper. What it said on religion was brief and relatively mild – obviously the ideologues had been too busy on more pressing subjects to pay much attention to believers: 'The right way to overcome religious prejudices is to heighten people's labour and social activity, educating them and devising and widely adopting new Soviet rituals.'[8]

The draft of the revised Party rules a week later did no more than instruct members to continue on the old path of 'resolute struggle' against religion.

Mr Gorbachev had been in power almost a year before he made his own first public pronouncement on the subject. This was at the 27th Party Congress on 25 February 1986. His meaning was far from clear: 'Stagnation is simply intolerable . . . in the entire sphere of ideological, political, labour, moral and atheistic upbringing . . . It is inadmissible to depict in idyllic terms reactionary, national and religious survivals contrary to our ideology.'[9]

When the Congress closed two weeks later, it added a caution regarding believers' feelings, one which had been uttered many times in the past, even though scant regard had been paid to it: 'The Party will use all forms of ideological influence for the wider propagation of a scientific understanding of the world, for the overcoming of religious prejudices without permitting any violation of believers' feelings.'[10]

Six months later *Pravda* published an editorial entitled 'To educate convinced atheists'. Again, the line was not strong, even though at that time, under its conservative editor, Viktor Afanasiev, it often lagged behind the pace of reform set by Mr Gorbachev. It touched upon recent debates in the Soviet press on the place of religion in literature and attacked 'flirting with god'. The hints that young people were still showing an interest in religion and the call for an intensification of atheist education were entirely conventional, merely repeating what had already been said a thousand times in the Soviet press over many years.

As was to be expected from a man who would become known as the arch reactionary in Mr Gorbachev's administration, when Yegor Ligachev came into the attack on 1 October 1986, addressing a conference of social scientists, he was much more specific:

> Sometimes when certain people encounter violations of socialist morality they begin to talk about the advisability of showing tolerance for religious ideas and of returning to religious morality. In doing so they forget the Marxist truism that religion can never be the source of man's moral principles. It was not religion that gave mankind the moral norms that are now shared by the human race . . . but by its content communist morality has significantly enriched the norms common to all mankind . . . Sometimes nationalism disguises itself in religious garb. This is clearly apparent, for example, in the reactionary element of the Islamic, Uniate and Catholic clergy. We must continue to search for new approaches, for new ways and means of atheist propaganda and work with believers.[11]

No words could make clearer the opposition that there would be in high places to the new deal which Mr Gorbachev would offer to believers eighteen months later. But before that offer, Gorbachev himself would take up Ligachev's challenge in what seems to have been his only major anti-religious statement. This came in an unexpected place, almost as a throw-away. On his way to India he stopped briefly in Tashkent on 24 November. Before a predominantly Muslim audience, he criticised the tendency of many writers to idealise the past and went on to attack many local officials, doubtless meaning those present, for compromising with religion by participating in religious rites. He continued with familiar and tired old phrases, saying there should be a 'decisive and uncompromising struggle' with religion and an improvement of atheist work in the republic. It is significant that the central press did not publish these remarks and they came to light only through a local newspaper. Was there some positive censorship in operation which deliberately excluded these anti-religious sentiments from gaining nationwide currency? Or was Mr Gorbachev pushed beyond what he had intended to say and himself attempted to limit the effect of his words after he had spoken them? The simplest and most likely explanation is to be found in the context. These words addressed militant Islam. They were never intended to be an attack against Christianity and therefore it would have been misleading to publish them in European Russia.

An article in *Izvestia* just a week later hinted that there might be a debate in the upper echelons of the Party, fuelled by the developments in Poland, where it was clear that the forces of atheism were gaining no ground whatsoever against the church.[12] The attack was against the role of the clergy in political life and its usurping of the role of guardian of and spokesman for the conscience of the nation. The clergy were seizing on the forthcoming Eucharistic Congress and visit of the Pope as a way of strengthening their influence on young people. The article quoted General Jaruzelski's views on the incompatibility of religion and communism.

Yevgeni Yevtushenko's article in *Komsomolskaya pravda*, the youth newspaper, struck a truly new note (see Chapter 1). He wrote of the aesthetic attraction of religious art and ritual and attacked the tendency to depict all discussion of religion as 'flirting with god'. Despite black spots in history, he continued, there were many instances of the church playing a progressive role. Finally, the adoption of atheism in no way guaranteed high standards of personal morality. These were much more likely to come from the general cultural standards in one's life.

This was the first salvo in a debate which began to go in a very interesting, not to say subversive, direction. Could it be that the promotion of atheism in itself was harmful to personal morality? A growing number of people seemed to think so and reflections of the debate began to appear in the Soviet press. If it were true, this would be another blow to the heartland of communism. After all, 'communist morality' had been a slogan of the system since the outset; the concept explicitly implied embracing Leninist atheism, so if it had set society on the wrong course, this was a condemnation of Lenin himself. Set beside the undoubted fact that a genuine religious revival was occurring in many different places, through which young people could see that conversion to Christianity did in reality bring in a new moral code, this article encouraged the beginning of a re-evaluation of attitudes which had become entrenched over seventy years.

New Role for the Church

Mr Gorbachev has always been an energetic traveller. He has, of course, wanted to meet and negotiate with influential foreign leaders, but he has also wanted to see other societies, including communist ones, for himself. This was much easier to arrange once he became leader. As an astute man, he can only have been forcibly struck by the immense difference between those countries which he had been brought up to think of as 'progressive' and those where 'man exploited man', in the phrase of the old dogma. He witnessed how not only was there no comparison between the standard of living of the two systems, but that the latter did, for all its defects and injustices, contribute overall to the dignity of mankind and to the establishment of prosperous social norms and an organised society. Even a tiny country like Iceland, with virtually no resources except fish in the sea and warm water flooding out of volcanic faults, and a climate no less harsh than many parts of the Soviet Union, could build up a prosperous and orderly people.

Increasingly, too, he saw with his own eyes the discontent which ordinary people living in socialist societies were beginning to express at the very time when, at last, they should have been enjoying some fruit from forty years of deprivation and rigorous control. What Gorbachev saw on Tienanmen Square in the summer of 1989 and then on the streets of East Berlin soon after must have contributed directly to his seeking an entirely new solution in the months immediately following.

One feature of his travels, almost entirely ignored by the world of secular journalism, was particularly significant. Almost everywhere he went, at least in the 'capitalist' world, he met church leaders. In Reykjavik Raisa Gorbachev visited a Lutheran church while her husband conferred. In Washington he met a circle of church leaders. In London, even during a visit lasting less than forty-eight hours, he met the Archbishop of Canterbury over a private lunch with the Queen. He also visited Westminster Abbey, where he heard the choir sing, a neat follow-up to his visit before he became leader, when he went to St Paul's Cathedral; his wife went to Christ Church Cathedral during their side trip to Oxford. At the state banquet at No.10 Downing Street I had the privilege of meeting him face to face. On 1 December 1989 came the most significant meeting of all, with the Pope at the Vatican (see Chapter 8), which led to the establishment of diplomatic relations between the Kremlin and the Vatican, a development whose speed no commentator could have predicted. The overall effect of visiting France, West Germany, Finland and other places must have been to demonstrate to Gorbachev that the church played a positive and dignified role within the very fabric of those societies.

At some stage in 1987, or more likely early in 1988, Mr Gorbachev came to a momentous decision: it was time to abandon the old dogma that religion was a retrogressive force, a relic of the past which could have no place in the future ideal communist society. When Karl

Marx had called it the 'opium of the people', he had not intended to damn it as a poison, but in the culture of the day, was using an image which represented temporary relief from pain. It seems unlikely that Mr Gorbachev was echoing Marx at this point and suggesting that, once again, religion could provide temporary relief from pain. His subsequent conduct showed a much more positive approach to religion than that and the effect of the new policies would be to develop the Yevtushenko debate and show religion to be a force for good in society.

As he looked around his vast and disparate agglomeration of republics, Mr Gorbachev could see that religion was alive and well. Believers were building within rather than tearing down the social fabric around them. The combination of religion and nationalism in such a vociferous form in Lithuania must have made him nervous, but even here there were signs of a society on the move, of people who originally wanted to make *perestroika* work. However, events moved so fast that by 1990 they were clearly intent only on immediate secession, not on helping the Soviet Union solve its other problems.

The Soviet system now desperately needed to find ways of turning words about 'restructuring' into deeds. The bureaucracy was as entrenched as ever and Mr Gorbachev could see resistance at all levels. After trying, with almost no success, to impose *perestroika* from above, could he find ways of inserting it into the system from below? It was too early to play the final card of inciting popular discontent against the system, but believers must have seemed to him a huge mass of neutral people who might be moved. There were tens of millions of them – figures are still unreliable, but it could be as many as 100 million, including Muslims, or more than one in three of the whole population. Because of the deliberate government policy of discriminating against the believer by blocking normal career opportunities, they occupied the most menial positions (though Christian workers, frequently loyal and conscientious, were not everywhere barred from exercising leadership on the shop floor and collective farm). If challenged in the right way, Mr Gorbachev must have reasoned, could they not be persuaded to move *perestroika* in at the bottom rung and start reforms at the local level, while above people still deliberated or even actively resisted?

If this was to happen, serious and genuine reforms in favour of religious liberty must come first. Somehow, trust and goodwill between individuals and groups must be re-established. There would have to be serious and deep concessions, not only an entirely new legislation, but, more difficult, the introduction of a new way of thinking among the ideologues of communism and the bureaucrats who maintained the system.

By a happy chance the timing was just right: the Millennium of the Orthodox Church was imminent. Already the state had given permission for the holding of a major international gathering in June 1988 to celebrate a thousand years of Christianity. The Danilov Monastery, returned to its rightful owners some five years previously, was beginning to look resplendent as the backcloth for an unprecedented drama.

Such must have been Mr Gorbachev's thinking as he considered what precise initiative he should take to implement his plan. He considered it was time to prepare new legislation and to make a promise to the leaders of the Orthodox Church.

At the same time as taking these steps, he had to find a formula which would, at least temporarily, satisfy the old guard. One was ready to hand – 'back to Lenin'. It is indeed true that on paper Lenin's legislation on religion looks much more liberal than the manifesto for persecution with which Stalin replaced it in 1929. Nevertheless, in practice the treatment believers received just after the Revolution was more than a foretaste of violence to come: by the time of Lenin's death in 1924 a full-scale persecution of Christians was under way.

While 'back to Lenin' was good enough for the conservatives, at least until they began to see drafts of the new legislation which made provision for the teaching of religion to children, it should not logically have satisfied believers. One suspects, however, that they were by this time so exhausted by the struggle for religious liberty that they took more notice of the tone of voice and the symbolism of the promotion of the Millennium celebrations on television and in the press than of the letter of Lenin's laws (not easily available for examination anyway). Early in 1988 the stage was set for the most portentous breakthrough for the church in Soviet history.

3 Orthodox Millennium

Mr Gorbachev and Patriarch Pimen

He never answered my letter. Instead, he did something better. Mr Gorbachev began, in 1988, to act as though he really did need believers to be in partnership with him in the massive task of rebuilding the moral basis of Soviet society.

I wrote to Mr Gorbachev, privately, in April 1987 and only when I received no reply did I publish the text. The central section of my letter challenged him to build a new relationship with believers:

> After seventy years of state atheism, constant pressure and even persecution, believers are still both a dynamic and a growing force in Soviet society. They are a major sector of the workforce. They do not want to overthrow: they want to construct something better from within. They have immense potential, given encouragement, to transform the social face of the land. They care intensely for their fellow human beings; they care for the values of society. They were of course grieved when, last year in Tashkent, you called for renewed and more effective measures to combat religion. However, were you to give a lead in a new direction, doubtless they would be ready to support you as Academician Sakharov has already done.
>
> If you give such a lead, you will be in a position to create a society such as the world has never known. But you would do more. If religious believers are free to play a genuine and positive role in your society, world peace will come a few steps closer, because your aims would be shared by millions of believers throughout the world – indeed, by the majority of the human race. There will be an entirely new dynamic in the struggle by the great powers to build a better world where resources go into third-world development and not into the arms race.[1]

Over thirty years I have become used to conducting a dialogue of the deaf with Soviet officialdom, but this time there was a reply, not in word but in deed. A year after my letter, church–state relations were transformed in the course of about eight weeks from April to June 1988. No one, least of all Soviet believers themselves, foresaw the drama that would unfold before the eyes of the world.

On 29 April 1988 a meeting unprecedented in post-war years took place. The setting was the grandiose Catherine Hall in the Kremlin. All official statements claim that Patriarch Pimen requested to see Mr Gorbachev to discuss the imminent Millennium celebrations. If indeed he acted so boldly, risking a rebuff, this would have been the most decisive action in his eighteen years of office, a period of passivity on the part of the Orthodox leadership remarkable even by comparison with the past. After all, Stalin had been dead nearly twenty years by the time of Pimen's election and other sectors of society were finding their voice as the terror receded into the past. For the church, memories of persecution were more recent, but they had only accentuated the will of believers to resist. The firm belief among the Orthodox intelligentsia in Moscow is that the Kremlin instigated the meeting, certainly to the extent of suggesting to the Patriarch that he should make a 'request' for it. The published information about it shows clearly that Mr Gorbachev was setting the agenda.

The only precedent for this event was when Stalin summoned Metropolitan Sergi to the Kremlin on 4 September 1943. Conditions, at least superficially, were then very different. It was in the darkest days of the war, when the Soviet Union, after a series of massive defeats at the hands of the Germans, was desperate to muster whatever resources it could. In return for loyalty and support in the war effort, both moral and financial (which indeed had already been forthcoming), Stalin would offer the church a reward if his forces achieved victory. He was as good as his word. The one-time seminarian who had devastated the church in the 1930s encouraged its material revival in the next decade.

Perhaps the moral mountain which Mr Gorbachev had to begin to climb in 1988 was no less precipitous and forbidding than the physical one which confronted Stalin in 1943. It is still, so close to the events, impossible to tell whether Mr Gorbachev's approach was in part prompted by some genuine sympathy for the church – a residual respect from his home background – or whether he acted as he did out of pure pragmatism. Whatever the truth, the decisiveness of his words matched the splendour of the setting and he probably had in mind the transformation which Stalin's meeting had achieved. The Patriarch and five attendant Metropolitans must have realised that history was about to unfold before their eyes.

Gorbachev's speech was statesmanlike, challenging and, within certain limitations, open and honest. He began by admitting the mistakes of the past:

> Not everything has been easy and simple in the sphere of church–state relations. Religious organisations were not free from being affected by the tragic developments that occurred in the period of the cult of personality. Mistakes made with regard to the church and believers in the 1930s and the years that followed are being rectified.[2]

The last sentence implied that unrectified mistakes had continued right up to the present, thus preparing the six church leaders for a decisive offer. According to Konstantin Kharchev, Chairman of the Council for Religious Affairs, who was present on the government side, Mr Gorbachev stated that 'the overwhelming majority of believers accept the policy of *perestroika*' and are contributing to economic improvements, to 'promoting democracy and *glasnost*'. There would be a tangible reward for this: 'A new law on freedom of conscience . . . will reflect the interests of religious organisations.' He continued:

> Believers are Soviet people, workers, patriots, and they have the full right to express their convictions with dignity. *Perestroika*, democratisation and *glasnost* concern them as well – in full measure and without any restrictions. This is especially true of ethics and morals, a domain where universal norms and customs are so helpful for our common cause.[3]

To hear the leader of the world's first atheist state, where the law restrained religious activity on all fronts, talk about 'our common cause' must have stunned these men who had themselves long been intimidated into political passivity and self-censorship. A more lapidary phrase was to follow, promising to dislodge a founding principle of Marxism-Leninism: 'We have a common history, a common motherland and a common future.' Unequivocally, Mr Gorbachev was abolishing the dogma of seventy years, which not even Stalin's concessions had permanently revised: that there would be no religious belief in the ideal socialist society of the future. The forthcoming Millennium celebrations, he continued, would cement believers with the whole population in supporting 'the great common cause of *perestroika* and the renewal of socialism'.

In a country which has no democracy there can be no real evidence to sustain or refute the claim that believers 'support the renewal of socialism'. A year later the elections to the Congress of People's Deputies of March 1989, and even more the local elections of 1990, would indicate widespread discontent at the dominance of the Communist Party, but one could not expect the church leaders to open up such a discussion at that point. Mr Gorbachev came now to the only palpably dishonest claim in the whole speech: that Lenin's decree on the separation of church and state of January 1918 allowed the church for the first time to conduct its activities 'without any outside interference'. We have seen that the exact opposite was true. Where the church is concerned, as with many other sectors of society, to insist on a return to 'Leninist norms' would compound, not solve, the problem. *Glasnost* has not yet approached the stage where it is possible openly to admit this, or even to re-examine the whole of historical evidence objectively, though there are signs that this is beginning to happen. Tactics, however, demanded that Mr Gorbachev should express some of the old principles with conviction, in order to allay the worst fears of his conservative opponents.

The Patriarch's reply put more emphasis on *perestroika* than on God. Indeed, He was not mentioned. Pimen pledged the unconditional support of believers for 'the architect of *perestroika*'. He would pray for the forthcoming summit meeting with President Reagan in Moscow. Already monasteries and churches were reopening and the 'pressing problems of church life' were being eased. For this he gave credit to the Council for Religious Affairs, which until recently had interfered daily in every aspect of church life and broken the constitutional edict that church and state must be separate. The Patriarch did not make a single request of the government or of Mr Gorbachev personally, though in discussion afterwards, according to the church's own account, they 'raised a number of specific questions associated with the guaranteeing of normal performance of the Orthodox Church'. There was no indication of what those questions were, but in formal speeches to Soviet officials during the Millennium celebrations the Patriarch, with evident emotion, twice referred to the profound impression the meeting with Mr Gorbachev had made on him.

The next month saw the Orthodox Church move centre stage in Russia and the world for the first time in the Soviet period. In May, the world's cameras followed President Reagan's footsteps as he met Christian and Jewish activists and when he visited the Danilov Monastery. The audience included millions of Soviet citizens themselves. In June the Soviet media reported every detail of the official Millennium celebrations. The famine of positive information about religion in the Soviet media suddenly became a glut: seventy lean years succeeded by something less than seventy fat days. When in my hotel room in Leningrad I switched on the TV, one channel was reporting the day's religious events; the other was relaying the recent film about Orthodox life, *Khram* ('Church'), which caught the atmosphere of worship with compelling beauty and a great reverence for Christian spirituality.

By visiting the Danilov Monastery on 30 May 1988, President Reagan turned his attention away from summitry to embrace publicly, as Mrs Thatcher had done at Zagorsk a year before him, the cause of religious liberty in the Soviet Union. There, in March 1987, she had lit a candle as a symbol of hope for those who were still being oppressed for their faith. Now there was an open monastery in Moscow for the first time since the 1920s. Curiously, it was Mr Andropov, former head of the KGB, or his staff who took the decision in 1983 to present the church with a dignified Moscow headquarters, where it could both host the Millennium celebrations five years later and gather within one complex all the main administrative divisions of the Moscow Patriarchate.

The monastery is enclosed within a massive wall. 'About right for a prison,' I mused in 1959 as I viewed its forbidding exterior while I was charting the open churches of Moscow. Entrance was barred then. Little did I know that inside was a Soviet borstal for young male offenders. Even less would I have guessed that thirty years later I would step inside to see it magnificently restored and awaiting the closing ceremony of the Millennium celebrations.

Due to a typical Soviet administrative error the first monks arrived before the young criminals had moved out. The two groups formed an immediate bond. Suffering from the standard treatment of offenders in the Soviet Union, the boys had never experienced any hint of love or care for them as individuals. The clergy, long before 'charity' was to become legal, spontaneously began to show their Christian compassion to a group who surely needed it.

When the boys moved out and restoration work began, the task was massive. Officially it cost 30 million roubles ($50m at the exchange rate then operating), but many believers in the Soviet Union think that the real figure was 50 million roubles. Even this is a subsidised total, because Christian volunteers helped in the massive task of clearing and reconstructing the site.

The magnificence of the restored monastery provided a foretaste of the imminent jubilee celebrations. While the timing of the Moscow summit cannot have been set to precede them by only a few days, the way events unfolded did seem to form part of some greater plan: the Russian Orthodox Church, having survived persecution, was poised to play a visible role on the world stage during its second millennium.

The Millennium Celebrations

The choice of Moscow as the focal point of the celebrations, before the guests departed to attend subsidiary events in other cities, was in itself controversial. After all, the city-state of Kiev had been the eye of medieval civilisation long before the foundation of Moscow and it was here that Prince Vladimir had descended the steep slope of the River Dnieper, ordering his courtiers and subjects to be baptised after him and to embrace the new faith. The river bore away the jettisoned idols and the images of paganism.

These events of 988 (though the date is a contested one among scholars) are considerably more than a folk memory. Partly as a result of the devastation of Kiev by the Golden Horde, the Asiatic invasion from the East, the focus of Russian civilisation shifted north; after the rise of Muscovy, Kiev declined in status and paid tribute to a new master. In time Kiev, restored to reflect the glory of its past, diverged in custom and language, eventually to become the capital of the emergent nation of Ukraine. Though part of the Russian and then, after a briefest spell of independence, of the Soviet empire, this vast region, with enormous economic resources, came to nurture a variety of anti-Moscow sentiments which were exacerbated by the growing insensitivity of the central government.

The choice of Moscow for the whole first week of celebrations (5–12 June) reminded Ukrainian believers that it was the Russian Orthodox Church which played the dominant role. It had even justified and benefited from the liquidation of the Ukrainian Catholic Church in Western Ukraine over forty years earlier (see Chapter 8), and it was now going to ensure that the focus was on Moscow. The rumblings about this below the surface – and they were not confined to Ukrainian nationalists – were an aspect of *glasnost* not aired in the Soviet press at the time. Certainly none of the 1,500 official guests from around the world and from other Soviet churches broke diplomatic protocol to raise such a sensitive issue publicly.

Sunday 5 June saw the opening liturgy in the Cathedral of the Epiphany, a building which had become the Patriarchal Cathedral after the eviction of the church from the Kremlin in 1917 and the destruction of the Cathedral of Christ the Saviour in 1934. For the second time in a week the world's television cameras recorded the splendour of Russian Orthodoxy at its most solemn and imposing. Christian leaders from many parts of the world joined in this ceremony, though ordinary believers would later complain at their exclusion from the main events.

The centre-piece of the whole event was the *sobor* (Council) which took place at the Holy Trinity Monastery at Zagorsk, to which we shall return later in the chapter.

I was due to arrive in Moscow on 7 June, not as an official guest, but as leader of a group of forty pilgrims coming to the Soviet Union under the auspices of Inter-Church Travel to join with Russians, Ukrainians and Belorussians in prayer and celebration of this most solemn event. In the few days before my departure I was a most unwilling participant in a personal drama which echoed around the British media.

All of our group received their visas well ahead of departure, with the exception of my wife and me. Mr Gorbachev and his *perestroika* had received very positive coverage in the world press as a result of the Moscow summit. Newsmen were only too ready afterwards to give prominence to any story which would make a negative point. In truth, the refusal of a visa to an individual was neither new (it had happened so often in the past) nor particularly newsworthy outside church circles. However, the way it was put made it sound more dramatic than it was. The 8 a.m. news on Radio 4 on 5 June introduced its leading item with the words: 'The Archbishop of Canterbury is in Moscow for the opening of the Millennium celebrations of the Russian Orthodox Church. However, one churchman who will not be accompanying him is . . .' Dr Runcie, furthermore, criticised the Soviet authorities for their refusal, which occasioned another wave of publicity a day later.

By the evening of Monday 6 June, the day before our scheduled departure, I had given up all hope and concluded that the combined efforts of the media, the travel agency (which threatened to cancel all future tours to the Soviet Union), the Foreign Office, the Archbishop and, not least, the prayers of many sympathisers had all failed.

But at 8.15 p.m. the phone rang to announce that our visas were ready and waiting for us at the Soviet Consulate. Our two-year-old son not only in the wrong bed, but in the wrong house, visas to be collected an hour's journey away, suitcases to be packed, departure at four next morning for a five-thirty check-in at Heathrow: all this domestic drama was soon forgotten in the joy of finally landing in Moscow and hearing our Intourist guide turn to an obstinate customs official with the words, 'These people are guests of the Patriarch; please let them through quickly.' What she said might not have been quite accurate, but the doors did spring open and we even spent part of the next day at the Holy Trinity Monastery, where the *sobor* itself was taking place.

On 7 June, the day I arrived in the Soviet Union, the Ukrainian Council of Ministers made a conciliatory gesture of major symbolic significance. In 1961 the authorities had expelled the monks from the great Monastery of the Caves in Kiev, a magnificent complex of buildings which linked the conversion of St Vladimir to the present. Nikita Khrushchev was surely aware that this would be one of the most brutally symbolic acts in his campaign to eradicate religion in the 'era of advanced communism' for which he believed he was preparing. History has a way with those who make extravagant claims. Khrushchev's decisive step towards the formulation of a religion-free society was reversed less than thirty years later. No single event of the Millennium could have been more pregnant with symbolism than the return of part of the Monastery of the Caves. A televised ceremony, during which the title deed was returned to Metropolitan Filaret of Kiev, gave it full publicity. If the state had not made this concession, the entire proceedings of the Millennium would have been tainted with hypocrisy.

The central drama of the week was hidden from the eyes of ordinary Russian believers and invited guests. The closed sessions of the *sobor* will go down in history as far more important than the combined weight of all the ceremonial occasions. *Sobor* is the Russian word for a gathering of people (a council) or for the building in which large numbers of worshippers meet (a cathedral). In practice a *sobor* meets only irregularly to transact business of extraordinary importance, especially the election of a new patriarch upon the death of the incumbent. Each diocese should send three representatives: the bishop, an elected priest and an elected layman.

The *sobor* of June 1988, which ran for four days (6–9 June) within the period of the Moscow Millennium celebrations, was the fourth in the Soviet period (counting the one already in session at the time of the 1917 Revolution), but the first which was not meeting for the election of a patriarch. When asked what was his single most abiding memory of an unforgettable occasion, Professor Sir Dimitri Obolensky replied in a single word, 'Laughter.' Far from being a flippant observation, this reveals the unimaginable change of atmosphere which had come about within the Russian Orthodox Church in so short a time.

The build-up which we have already described led to an expectancy in the air, a sense of quiet joy that something had so visibly changed in favour of the church. Walking around the Holy Trinity Monastery as I did on the day of the closed session (8 June), one could sense this among those whom we met and who were on the fringes of this great event. There could have been no greater contrast than the atmosphere of the previous *sobor* of 1971, which elected Patriarch Pimen. Here the aim of the Soviet authorities had been to dominate the proceedings by the silent presence of the representatives of the Council for Religious Affairs. Would-be dissenting bishops had been prevented from attending by physical attacks on their persons; regulations restricting the participation of clergy in the administrative and financial affairs of their own parishes had been illegitimately in place for a decade and this assembly of 1971 had to formalise the status of these; the *sobor* had to 'elect' a quiescent patriarch whose unopposed candidature was virtually signed and sealed before the event.

By 1988 it was time for the *sobor* to regain its dignity and self-respect. That it went so far towards achieving this is a milestone in the history of the Russian Church. The laughter was only one sign of a spontaneity about the proceedings which was something new under Soviet conditions. The best illustration of this came with two acts of 'charity' which, even at that time, were still technically illegal.

On the Saturday immediately before the opening of the Millennium celebrations (4 June) there had been a rail crash and the detonation of a truck of high explosives at Arzamas, near Gorky. In accordance with the new policy of open reporting in the press, the news immediately went round that sixty-eight people had died in the explosion and several hundred others were injured. Someone organised a collection at the *sobor* for the victims, which realised no less than 50,000 roubles. If, say, there were 500 people in the room (there were probably fewer), the average contribution was £100 sterling per person at the official rate of exchange. At the very end of the *sobor* there was a requiem for the dead in the Afghan War, in itself an unprecedented event, as the churches had always been barred from publicly praying for any victims of Soviet adventurism. The collection at this service amounted to no less than four times the contribution for the rail disaster.

The opening and closing days of the *sobor* were largely ceremonial and the foreign guests were present. The closed sessions contained much more of significance and it has become possible to reconstruct the main events, as the press office made available the texts of the most important speeches. There are no transcripts of the ensuing discussions, so one is dependent on hearsay evidence for some of what took